HARRY'S GAME

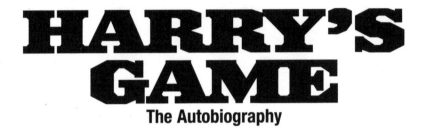

HARRY'S GAME

The Autobiography

Harry Gregg with Roger Anderson

Additional research: Andy Walsh

MAINSTREAM
PUBLISHING

EDINBURGH AND LONDON

Dedication

Roger Anderson: In memory of my mum Amy Anderson

First published in Great Britain in 2002 by
MAINSTREAM PUBLISHING COMPANY (EDINBURGH) LTD
7 Albany Street
Edinburgh EH1 3UG

ISBN 1 84018 366 7

A catalogue record for this book is available from the British Library

Typeset in Baskerville and Garamond

Printed in Great Britain by
Butler & Tanner Ltd, Frome and London

CONTENTS

FOREWORD BY GEORGE BEST

The term hero is a much-overused one in football and in life generally. But Harry Gregg is an authentic hero in the true sense of the word, although the measure of the man is that he would never ever consider the notion.

I first met Harry on the training ground in 1961 when I was a wisp of a lad arriving at Manchester United for the first time. It was my greatest thrill to meet him in the flesh, as back in Northern Ireland he was the player revered by all football fans more than any other – no mean feat for a goalkeeper. One reason was because he had been part of the most successful national football side in Irish history when they battled through to the last eight of the 1958 World Cup finals and the other because he kept goal for Manchester United, the English club supported by more Irish people than any other.

Sir Matt Busby pushed us together straight away because he thought that Harry would be a steadying and parental influence on me and perhaps banish any thoughts I might have had of disappearing back to the comfort of my family, home and friends in Belfast. I was struck by the sheer size of him but he put me at my ease immediately with his kindness and gentle manner. I considered it an honour to be given the task of cleaning his boots (such were the chores of the apprentice in those days). He really was respected and loved at the club. Not only had he survived the Munich air crash in which so many of his teammates and friends perished but he had bravely gone back into the burning wreckage of the aeroplane to rescue a young woman, her baby and others. As I got older and talked to various people still at the club who were there that fateful night, the enormity of Harry's actions sunk in and he continued to rise in my estimation. Bravery is one thing – all goalkeepers must have it to a certain degree – but what Harry did that night was about more than just bravery. It was about goodness.

By the time I became established in the team Harry's best playing days were behind him. He was a fantastic goalkeeper, as good in the air as he was on the ground, and a joy to watch. But he was plagued by a shoulder injury that meant he often played in extreme pain and if it did impair his performance no one noticed. After he retired from the game he always kept in contact. He still does. Harry has been a true friend to my father in Ireland, visiting him and ringing regularly to chat and see how the old fella is doing and he has always contacted me to offer help and friendship when I have been ill or hospitalised. I know Harry, like my father, was worried during my darkest days but, like my Dad, he would never have presumed to tell me how to live my life.

Harry Gregg was a great athlete and is a great man. Harry, you're my hero – and I mean that.

George Best
Surrey, England
Summer 2002

I

TOBERMORE TO TRAFFORD

Every morning I get up around seven, pull on an old tracksuit and head for Portstewart Strand. It is on this crescent stretch of sand, with the roar of the Atlantic rollers for company, that I feel most alive. No doubt it is a legacy of my playing days, but even now I feel the need to keep in shape. Maybe there is still a footballer in there desperately trying to get out.

It is during this splendid isolation that I reflect on my life. Much of it has been played out on the pages of newspapers, but that has only handed people a distorted picture of who I am. I've no doubt there are many who see me as a bolshie sort of bloke with a stubborn streak as long as the Strand I like to stroll. But they don't really know me. Sure I've always believed in fighting my corner. And yes, I've often spoken out when the diplomatic thing would have been to keep my mouth shut, or hit out when others might have counted to ten. But there have also been many occasions when I've bitten my tongue, never more so than over Munich.

In the years since Munich I've come across people who have a strange kind of morbid jealousy of those who were involved in the crash. Well, if they want to be part of it, they can have the horror that goes with it. They can have mine. I've listened to half-truths, outright lies. I've read newspaper articles and books purporting to tell the real Munich story. And I've remained silent when others who were present have altered their version of events to such an extent that I have to pinch myself and ask: 'Was I really there?' After the crash I was dubbed the Hero of Munich. That notoriety has come at a price. For Munich has succeeded in casting a shadow over my life that I've found difficult to dispel. I might have escaped the wreckage on that runway in Germany, but from that day to now there has been no escape. Despite what I achieved before and since as a footballer, and as a man, it is Munich, and Munich alone, for which I am best remembered by many. Every anniversary the phone calls start. It doesn't matter if I don't feel like re-opening the wounds, Harry Gregg, Hero of Munich, has somehow become public property.

Munich shaped my destiny, of that there is no doubt. But Munich is not my life. When I close my eyes and breathe in that crisp early morning air I also think about great teams, great players, great games. I think of moments of undiluted joy and gut-wrenching personal loss, of laughing in the company of wonderful characters and crying salty tears in solitude. And if there is one thing I've learned in this life, it is never to take life for granted.

That lesson was learned at an early age. I was born on 27 October 1932, in the village of Tobermore. The first of six children, I was older brother to Wesley, Elizabeth, Billy, Denis (who died at the age of two) and Kenneth. Anything I have achieved in my life pales in comparison to the stoicism shown by my brother Billy. At five years old he contracted polio and lost the use of his legs. Billy was taken away from us and for 15 years he led a miserable existence in a home where neglect was a part of everyday life. Deprived of a set of crutches, the only way he could get about was to crawl. Many would have found the nearest corner and wasted away, but Billy chose instead to educate himself and eventually he set up a small business repairing shoes. Billy drives me nuts talking about football. He's an intelligent fellah and I'm very proud to call him my brother. I suppose it was inevitable, but there was plenty of sibling rivalry in our house. Though I can tell you this, I'd have taken all my brothers on rather than tackle our Elizabeth. Growing up around us lads, she certainly learned to stand up for herself.

My father came from a staunch loyalist family. My mum Isobel, on the other hand, came from a strong Catholic family. I suppose it is what we call today a mixed marriage. Once it was clear that my mum and dad were serious about each other, her family disowned her. I never had, and never will have, time for that kind of bigotry. As far as I'm concerned it is each to their own, just as long as no one is trying to force their views on me.

Once I talked Mum into attempting a reconciliation, but it fizzled out. Even the passage of time hadn't healed the bitterness.

The Gregg family eventually moved to Windsor Avenue in Coleraine and it was there that I spent my teenage years. It was a time I look back on with great fondness. At the top of our street stood Victoria Park, an expanse of lush grassland. Every available minute was spent there, especially during the summer months. When winter closed in we played football under the street lights, goal posts daubed on walls. It proved ideal preparation for my time at United when we would go up to the back of the Stretford End to play five-a-sides on the cinders between Old Trafford's floodlight pylons. When you're brought up on street football the thought of diving around on rock-hard surfaces holds little fear.

When the Second World War broke out the authorities situated the underground shelters beneath Victoria Park. When hostilities ended, prefabs took the place of shelters and a wonderful greenfield site was lost forever. Still, with Coleraine's ground just 150 yards from my front door, football was inescapable. The game occupied all my thoughts and dreams. And like most youngsters I had an idol. His name was Johnny Thomson. A goalkeeper with Glasgow Celtic, I'd read about his exploits in *Thompson's Weekly*, a leading sports paper of the time. Johnny was tragically killed in 1931 during an Old Firm match. As he dived at the feet of the on-rushing Rangers player he was kicked in the head and suffered a fractured skull. I'd never seen him play, yet his legend lived on in the printed word and, thanks to one local man, in song. Any time there was a party, Chinny Brown would give his rendition of an ode to Johnny Thomson – *Johnny Thomson was a miner, he came from Canarden, he joined the Glasgow Celts, to make himself a name.* Considering my upbringing I should have been a Glasgow Rangers fan, but Johnny was my hero and because of him, Celtic were my team.

The less said about my school days the better. I wasn't expelled, but let's just say my mother thought it a good idea to move me to Coleraine Model. On my arrival I was horrified to find that there was no provision for sport of any kind at the school – that was until Mr McDonald joined the teaching staff. A distinguished-looking gent, with his neat pin-striped suits and horn-rimmed glasses, Mr McDonald introduced football and I began my playing career as a left-back. It wasn't long, though, before I found myself between the sticks, the move initiated out of fear for the safety of my teammates. I think it was fair to say I was a little rough and ready in those days. I took to my new-found position like a duck to water, so much so that Mr McDonald recommended me for Irish Schoolboy trials. I was only 13 and it broke my heart when I reached the final trial but wasn't selected.

The following year my parents put my name down for the entrance exam at Coleraine Academical Institution, a grammar school with a tradition for sporting and academic excellence. They had high hopes that I would be the first Gregg to tread its hallowed corridors. I had other ideas. With rugby and cricket dominating the extra-curricular activities, I conspired to flunk the exam and head instead to the football-playing Coleraine Technical College. It wasn't a bad decision on my part, for the following year I was chosen to captain Ireland Schoolboys against Wales. It wasn't all good news, though, for here I was living a stone's throw from Coleraine Football Club, captaining my country, and yet I couldn't even get a second glance from my hometown team. What made matters worse was that another lad from the town, Davy McClelland, had been signed by Coleraine on the strength of his selection for the international schoolboys team.

I was never starved of football, though. The junior scene (junior being something of a misnomer as this was adult football) more than adequately filled the gap left by Coleraine Football Club's apathy. Coleraine Villa were the leading junior team around, boasting players like Frank 'Bunty' Montgomery, who would go on to be capped at both amateur and full international level. I was desperate to play for the Villa. However, as I was walking through the town centre one day I was stopped by a bloke called Jim Leighton and asked to join a team he was forming. Ironically, Coleraine Wanderers would go on to become the Villa's biggest rivals. Still in my early teens, I combined youth football with sides like Ballymoney YMCA (where I won my first Boys Clubs international cap) and regular appearances in the South Derry League. Playing with your peers was one thing, but this was something else again. As a young lad of 15 with Claughey United I quickly learned that few allowances would be made for my tender years. If anybody did take liberties, regardless of which team I was playing for, they soon found out that the beanpole in goal had his own minders in the shape of experienced campaigners Bobby Brown, Frankie Trainor, Ned O'Kane, and Mickey Mullan. Retribution was close at hand.

I knew I had talent, but making the grade in football isn't always about ability. Luck, too, can play a part. Take my debut for Coleraine Reserves as a 14-year-old. With nothing in my pockets but fluff, I decided to climb over the wall to avoid paying to see the match with Linfield's second string (known as the Swifts). No sooner had my feet touched the ground than I was grabbed by the scruff of the neck. Collared by the groundsman, I was already thinking about how I would explain this to my mum when he led me into the home dressing-room. I needn't have worried. The next thing I knew the reserves manager Jim White was asking if I had a pair of boots because they were a man short. I didn't, but I knew a man who did. I sprinted around to Melvin McCaw's house as if my life depended on it, borrowed his boots and played in goal. It wasn't the most auspicious of debuts. We lost 4–1! I did get 15 shillings for my efforts, but that was scant consolation for the indifference shown towards me after the match by the Coleraine officials. I thought I'd lost out on my big chance to impress. I was wrong. A week later two men appeared at my front door and asked if I knew where to find young Gregg the goalkeeper. One was Joe Bambrick, the famous Northern Ireland international. A scoring phenomenon, Joe entered the record books in 1930 when he helped himself to six goals in a 7–0 win over Wales at Celtic Park. The other man was Linfield official Jack Smith. They said that after enquiring with the Irish League and Irish Football Association they'd learned I wasn't on Coleraine's books. I told them Coleraine had never asked and was chuffed to bits when they offered me the chance to sign amateur forms for Linfield Football Club.

The Blues (Linfield) were Northern Ireland's equivalent of Glasgow Rangers, so I signed on the dotted line and twice a week made the 120-mile round trip to Belfast. The rest of the time I continued the apprenticeship I'd started as a joiner. I played my first match for Linfield Swifts (the reserve team) as a 15-year-old against Ballymoney United, a junior team just eight miles up the road from my home. And my spell at Linfield was only a few weeks old when I received the first of what would become a painstakingly compiled catalogue of injuries. I broke bones in my wrist and the hospital told me I had to stay in plaster for 13 weeks. But, after just six, doctor Gregg thought he knew better. I had been informed of my selection to play for the youth team in a tournament in Liverpool and there was no way I was going to miss the opportunity. So, with no little difficulty, I prised the plaster cast off my arm and crossed the Irish Sea. I played in three matches and at my next doctor's appointment told the understandably sceptical medic that the cast had just slipped off. Not the most convincing excuse in the world and he sent me back to the hospital to have it replaced.

My time with Linfield ended on something of a sour note. The Swifts were scheduled to play an important cup tie and I was fully expecting to start. At Windsor Park the custom was for the starting 11 to place their boots on the relevant peg in the dressing-room. I was the man in possession at the time and had no inkling of what was about to happen. My challenger for the role as the club's number two keeper was a chap called Hughie Friel. Hugh had been recently signed from Sion Mills and having glanced at the pegs, he stormed off. Minutes later a club official walked in, lifted my boots off and told me I wasn't playing. I can understand Hughie wanting to play, we all do in these situations, but I was seething at my treatment.

It was hard to see just how my career with Linfield could progress and I sat the police entrance exams in the expectation that one day I might have to find a career outside the game. Fortunately, Coleraine had clearly been watching my progress and a local character called Mickey McColgan asked me would I consider signing for them. Mickey was an amazing wee man. Small in stature but with the heart of a lion, he would use bare-faced cheek and the gift of the gab to open doors. In fact, during the Second World War he managed to persuade several top English players who were stationed in Ulster (like Sunderland's international Billy Elliot) to sign for

Coleraine. After initially ignoring me, my hometown team now thought that if I was good enough for Linfield, I was good enough for them.

Mickey took me along to see the club chairman Sammy Walker. Sammy, who would later become president of the Irish Football Association, was one of the game's genuine authorities. He continued to follow my career from that day on and was a friend and confidant I feel fortunate to have known. Coleraine offered me £80 to join them, plus three pounds and ten shillings a week in wages. It was less than I was making as a joiner, but then being a chippy wasn't my ambition, playing football was. I took the signing-on fee straight home to my mother. I suppose it was an early example of being tapped. Even at amateur level it happened, anyone who thought otherwise wasn't living in the real world.

One of the incentives for signing was the promise of first-team football. The consequence of that promise was someone else's misfortune. Irish Amateur international Jim Watt was the man set to be dropped in favour of a lad still wet behind the ears. I was never going to win any dressing-room popularity polls and the supporters weren't exactly falling over themselves to extend the hand of friendship when my debut ended in a 5–1 defeat by Ards. It might sound daft but I blamed a visit to the local barber's for the result. I'd been so anxious to look the part on my big day I'd gone for a haircut at Jim King's. It was the first and last time in my career that I ever had a haircut on match day.

Not surprisingly, Coleraine's management didn't dare play me in the next match. In fact, it was nine weeks before I returned to first-team action. When I did, things really started to click. First, I was selected for an international youth tournament in Monte Carlo, then I replaced Jim in the Irish Amateur side. I was 18, my name was now receiving mention in dispatches and I had a gilt-edged chance to impress further when I was included in an Irish League XI to play our English counterparts. With the English team boasting the likes of Nat Lofthouse, Tom Finney and Billy Wright, this was the closest thing possible to a full international. The night before the match I didn't get much sleep. It wasn't nerves which kept me awake, it was just I couldn't believe my luck.

My departure from Windsor Park and that ignominious debut for

Coleraine now seemed irrelevant. I was well and truly on my way, or so I thought. The reality of the situation, however, was anything but the stuff of boyhood dreams. Our centre-forward managed ten touches – once when he tapped the ball at kick-off and another nine after each of the English goals. All of this in front of a packed Windsor Park. I just wanted the ground to open up and swallow me.

I was convinced my fledgling career was in ruins, but over the coming months there was talk linking me to Glasgow Rangers and Manchester United. Coleraine's chairman, Jack Doherty, also told me that Burnley wanted me on a month's trial. I passed the information on to our manager, ex-Scottish international Arthur Milne, but he refused to let me go. Arthur felt that if I was good enough to cross the Irish Sea, it should be on a permanent basis. The Turf Moor management didn't pursue their interest, but I didn't have long to wait before I was packing my bags for good. The man who signed me, Doncaster Rovers' boss Peter Doherty, was to have a profound influence on me. Peter the Great, as he was known among his contemporaries, was the most talented player ever to leave the Emerald Isle. He was perpetual motion, with incredible stamina which carried his slender frame effortlessly from box to box. And there was also a craft and invention about his play which few, if any, have surpassed. Dazzling in an era blessed with brilliance, Doherty's displays prompted ex-England international turned *Evening Standard* writer Bernard Joy to say: 'There were some great inside forwards – Raich Carter, Wilf Mannion, Bryn Jones, Tommy Walker, Billy Steel – but I rate Peter Doherty'the best of them all.'

I was working for Jack Doherty as a joiner on a site in Portstewart when I was told to go to Coleraine Showgrounds. Jack was there with Peter and I stood there in awe as the great man was given the hard sell. Jack said: 'The boy can throw the ball out to the halfway line,' neglecting to add that I was also barely able to kick it beyond my own 18-yard box. Doncaster signed me for £1,200, with a further £500 after a dozen first-team appearances. And I actually took a pay cut to move. My wages from Coleraine and earnings as a joiner came to the princely sum of £11 – Doncaster paid £6 a week in the summer, £7 in the winter. Money, though, was of little importance and I would gladly have handed every penny back to Peter for the honour of playing for him. Moving to working-class Yorkshire might not sound like much of a transition to make, but, believe me, this was a whole new world. I stayed with Bill Patterson and Tommy Martin, both lads making this shy Ulsterman feel right at home. I'll never forget Tommy saying to me that there was £40 in the top drawer in his room and that if ever I needed a few quid I was to help myself. Bill was a centre-half with a burgeoning reputation and it wasn't long before Newcastle United forked out £22,500 and whisked him off to Tyneside. In fact, it was thanks to Bill's progress that I had my first experience of Old Trafford. We had become quite friendly before his move north and when I found out he was playing for the Magpies against Manchester United I went along and stood at the Stretford End to watch. I never imagined that one day the fans would be there watching me.

Doncaster Rovers may have slipped down the divisions over the decades, but they were no Mickey Mouse club in the early 1950s. Within weeks of my arrival at Belle-Vue a Doncaster Rovers Select XI played a team of ex-internationals under floodlights. Rovers were one of the first clubs in England to install lights and I found the whole occasion of a night match totally intoxicating. With the cold air condensing the spectators' breath into a fine mist, the stillness of the night and the illuminating rays from the floodlights, there was a magical quality to proceedings. The ground was packed and the opposing team bursting with household names. As I stood there watching Frank Swift, Raich Carter, Joe Mercer and Peter Doherty, it only confirmed my romantic preconception of football in England. Two weeks later and I was experiencing the unique night-match atmosphere from between the sticks, donning Doncaster colours for the first time in a friendly with the team I'd supported as a boy, Glasgow Celtic.

I played in Rovers Reserves for two or three months before making my first-team debut on 24 January 1953, against Blackburn Rovers. We were 2–0 up at half-time, but my luck ran out just after the re-start and I found myself back in the dressing-room after dislocating my elbow in a collision with my own full-back and Blackburn's centre-forward Tommy Briggs.

Keen to impress, I'd made a suicidal dive for the ball. Looking back it could have ended my career in England before it had really begun. Two St John's ambulancemen had to hold me down whilst Mr Semple, a doctor and one of the club's directors, struggled to put my elbow back in. With the job done and me sweating buckets thanks to the excruciating pain, I was handed a blanket and left sitting. I needed medical attention but in those days you had to wait until the match was over to see a doctor. When I did finally reach hospital, I was told I had also chipped bones in both my upper and lower arm. The doctor demanded to know who had 'reduced it', explaining that it should never have happened without anaesthetic. More worryingly, he said the elbow injury was potentially career-threatening. However, thanks to the help of a friend, Bill Gold (a keeper with Wolverhampton Wanderers during Stan Cullis' heyday), I was back in the side by April. By the end of the season, I was the regular first-team keeper. As for the elbow, well, I still can't straighten the damn thing.

Post-season I returned home, pleased to be able to say I was really making progress. I wasn't upwardly mobile for long. I went out for a kickabout with some of the lads I'd grown up with and, Sod's law, broke my foot. By the time I'd reached home I was in agony. By the time I'd left hospital I was in plaster cast again. The doctors said 16 weeks' rest, but just to prove I hadn't grown any more sensible with age, I was up to my old tricks again after just one month. I wanted to get back to Doncaster for the start of the season, so I tried kicking a ball, plaster cast *et al.* It didn't feel too bad, so I cracked the plaster just before I was due to see the doc in the hope he'd finish the job and remove it. My ruse worked a treat, right up to the point where the doctor said my injury hadn't healed and applied a fresh cast. I wasn't finished and responded with the old soften-the-plaster-with-hot-bath routine. Then, using a hammer and chisel, I removed the source of my irritation. I strapped the foot in crepe bandages and caught the next boat to England. Peter went ballistic when he saw me and packed me off to the radiologist. He verified that I should still be in plaster. I, in turn, argued that jumping on and off ferries and buses to get here proved it wasn't that bad. In the end we compromised. He wouldn't force me to wear the cast and I would confine myself to walking until he gave me the nod. For all my efforts I never did start that season in goal. I think, though, that Peter realised my impatience stemmed from a genuine love of football. We failed to see eye to eye on a few occasions, although I was never outspoken or cheeky. Peter insisted that all the Doncaster first team lads play 36 holes of golf on a Thursday afternoon and I point blank refused. I told the boss that I didn't come to England to be a golfer and instead I went off to practise my goal-kicks. To be honest I always felt there was a certain affinity between us. And I'm proud to say that not long after his death, Peter's wife Jessie told me how he ranted and raved about my antics, then confessed he saw something of himself in me.

While I was making my name with Doncaster, Matt Busby was busy moulding his second great team just over the Pennines. In 1949 Busby had defied convention by dovetailing established players with a band of promising youngsters. Had Alan Hansen been a pundit at the time he'd probably have informed Matt he'd never win anything with kids, yet, after only three years' nurturing, they won United a League Championship. Led by Johnny Carey, aided and abetted by the likes of Jack Rowley, Henry Cockburn, Stan Pearson and Jimmy Delaney, this was a side capable of producing the most mesmerising football.

Now, with some of his most influential players beginning to age, Busby set about some dramatic squad surgery. Youthful exuberance has always been at the heart of United's most successful sides. Now it was the turn of another squad of players to pull on the red shirt and approach matches with the sort of unfettered play that is the club's hallmark. Things were beginning to click by 1956. United were going great guns in the league, although their FA Cup run was cut short courtesy of a 4–0 thumping by Bristol Rovers. As luck would have it, Doncaster were paired with the Red Devils' conquerors in the next round. We played out of our skins to win and, with Bristol Rovers' defeat of Manchester United attracting the Movietone cameras, I sneaked into a cinema to see myself on the screen for the first time. There was no stopping Busby's team in the league, though, and successive championships made their way to Old Trafford.

I, too, would soon be on the move. The question was, to which club? Charlton Athletic, Burnley, Aston Villa and Bolton Wanderers had all expressed interest in me, with Wolves manager Stan Cullis going as far as to have a chat with Peter. It was Sheffield Wednesday, though, who were the most up front in declaring their desire to sign me. A firm bid of £18,000 was tabled, with the suggestion that the Yorkshire club might even go higher. I definitely harboured ambitions to play in the top flight, but there was also a sense of loyalty to Doncaster Rovers and the fans who had taken me to their heart. The Belle-Vue faithful had followed the transfer talk in the press and they besieged the club with calls asking me to stay. Deep down, though, I knew that my days in Yorkshire were numbered.

Before joining Doncaster, I had sworn never to return to Ireland a failure. I even had a contingency plan, jotting down the address of Australia House and taking it with me to England. Believe it or not, I still have that frayed piece of paper today. When I look at it I'm reminded of just how fine the line is between success and failure. But succeed I had, and Manchester United were just about to make me the world's most expensive goalkeeper.

II

CAVANAGH'S CRYSTAL BALL

It was in the medical room at Belle-Vue after morning training that Doncaster's physio Jack Martin passed on the message. Short and sweet, he told me to report back at two o'clock. With so much transfer speculation in the papers my mind was doing cartwheels. I knew something was up, a feeling reinforced on my arrival when the reserves player-coach Jack Hodgson sent me across the pitch to the airport side of the ground and through the turnstile to where an estate car was waiting. It was all cloak-and-dagger stuff as I clambered into the back and a blanket was thrown over my head. The car then drove through Doncaster to Peter Doherty's house for a meeting with Matt Busby and Jimmy Murphy.

I suppose you could say it was fate, for only a few weeks earlier I'd been sitting watching United play Birmingham on a black and white TV in my mate Tommy Cavanagh's front room. Tommy pointed to United on the television screen and said: 'You're too good for the Second Division, that's where you should be, playing with the likes of them.' It had been the Doncaster board which had resurrected the United deal. After initially refusing to sell, understandable considering our precarious league position, they had a sudden change of heart. A meeting of the Board of Directors was convened at Belle-Vue, coinciding with Manchester United's Youth Cup match with Leeds United at Elland Road. Events were now gathering pace.

When I arrived at 69, Chestnut Avenue, Peter's wife Jessie made a cup of tea and left us to it. Peter told me United were interested, but Doncaster wanted me to stay. I think by this stage his attempt at persuading me to remain at Belle-Vue was nothing more than a token gesture. Then the doorbell rang and in walked Matt Busby and Jimmy Murphy. Peter went straight for the jugular: 'Right, Matt, the boy's ready to sign!' Busby wasn't going to be rushed. He wanted to hear from the horse's mouth. 'Son, do you want to sign for Manchester United?' Without a second's hesitation I replied: 'Yes!' 'We don't pay a signing-on fee. Do you still want to sign?' Once again I dived in. 'Yes!' I said, and I meant it. The following day I caught the train to Manchester, where my welcoming committee consisted of Matt Busby, Jimmy Murphy, Jackie Blanchflower, Jean Blanchflower and what appeared to be every press man in Britain.

It wasn't just that I was signing for Manchester United, but also that the transfer fee was a world record for a goalkeeper. Now, I'm sure £23,500 looks paltry set against today's megabucks game. And, yes, I know David Beckham probably spends more on haircuts, but to be the most expensive goalkeeper in the world was a source of pride to me – still is. Jackie Blanchflower told me later that Matt Busby had quizzed him about me. Jackie said he thought I was the best goalkeeper in the world. But Matt said: 'No, I'm not talking about his ability, we'll take care of that. I'm asking about his character.' To me that typified Matt and the philosophy of Manchester United at the time. Busby and Murphy weren't just interested in building a team, they wanted to build a club. Alex Ferguson did the same in the 1990s. He questioned whether players had that something special which he felt qualified them to play for Manchester United.

In 1957 I was joining a team which had enjoyed tangible success. It was a team, though, that was just starting to fray around the edges. The previous season United had played a total of 57 matches, losing only 9 and scoring a record 143 goals into the bargain. The following campaign kicked off in a similar vein. First Manchester City were beaten 1–0 in the Charity Shield, then the league began with five wins on the bounce and a solitary draw. Suddenly, without warning, the wheels started to come off. United went on a downward spiral culminating in just one win in the next four. And it was the nature of those defeats. Arch-rivals Bolton Wanderers scored four without reply, Blackpool took maximum points at Old

Trafford and Wolves made home advantage count with a comfortable 3–1 win. Matt Busby wasn't panicking, but the alarm bells were ringing. Having only lost six matches the entire season before, by December the loss column read seven. The usually dependable Ray Wood was suffering a crisis of confidence, no doubt the legacy of the broken cheekbone he sustained in the FA Cup final.

Goalkeepers in the modern game are a protected species. In 1957, it was the law of the jungle. The shoulder charge was an accepted part of the game and at Wembley my international colleague Peter McParland wreaked havoc with it. Peter had just headed the ball towards goal, where it was comfortably collected by Ray Wood. Television pictures confirm that Peter hit Ray front on with his shoulder. Peter, who, I must point out, was a fierce competitor, but not a dirty player, then inadvertently smashed into Ray's face with his head. Jackie Blanchflower took over in goal as Ray Wood received treatment from United's physio Ted Dalton. When he had recovered his senses, Ted took Ray to a strip of grass outside the tunnel entrance to the stadium. A young lad eager for a kickabout and blissfully unaware that they were major players in the drama unfolding inside, promptly asked if they fancied a game. The offer was declined and Woody rejoined his teammates for the second-half. Clearly unfit to continue in goal, he was dispatched to the wing. As if to rub salt in the wound, Peter McParland went on to score two, his second clearly offside. When Tommy Taylor pulled a goal back, Woody returned to the nets, but the equaliser never came. Manchester United were a shoulder charge away from becoming the first team that century to do the Double.

Matt had already recognised the need for changes as Christmas neared. He wouldn't tolerate a further slide down the table and on 21 December 1957, before the home match with Leicester City, he took everyone by surprise by dropping five first-team regulars – Ray Wood, Jackie Blanchflower, Johnny Berry, David Pegg and Liam Whelan – in favour of Bobby Charlton, Mark Jones, Kenny Morgans, Albert Scanlon and me! The unfortunate quintet left kicking their heels on the sidelines were the very men who had played a pivotal role in winning two championships. Reputations counted for little with Matt, though, and he felt it was time to shake them up a bit. Squad rotation may be commonplace today, but not in the '50s. Matt Busby not only shuffled his pack, he also did so with the calculated courage of a card sharp. Though some doubted him, he never wavered. In fact, on the Saturday following the match with Leicester, United's Reserve team that played Barnsley contained no less than 10 internationals.

Despite what many people thought, Matt Busby was not obsessed with winning the European Cup. No doubt it was to become his Holy Grail, but not yet, as this quote from him confirms: 'We would like to win the European Cup, of course, but above all I would like to win the English League Championship for the third year in succession. Herbert Chapman achieved this with Huddersfield and Arsenal, and it is the ultimate peak for any manager.' He was, though, already formulating a strategy to at least give us a chance to join the party. Matt watched as United's domestic success attracted interest on the Continent. And he demonstrated his determination to eventually pursue his European vision by rejecting a £65,000 Inter Milan bid for Tommy Taylor. He was worried, though. The lira-laden Italian clubs could offer terms that no one in England could match due to maximum wage regulations, and he had warned that unless the restriction was abolished our best players would move abroad.

The New Year saw us attacking on two fronts. On 4 January, league concerns were put on hold as I travelled with the team to Workington for my first FA Cup tie in United colours. They may be non-league today, but in 1958 they had a helluva team. They had a South African called Ted Purdon at centre-forward. Big Ted liked to hurt goalkeepers for fun. Throw into the mix Bobby Mitchell and their record-signing Ken Chisholm, and there was plenty of cause for concern. Workington started strongly, backed by a record gate of 21,000. At the end of 45 minutes they led 1–0. Enter Dennis Viollet. Dennis was on a real hot scoring streak and spent the second-half setting up his teammates and hitting a hat-trick himself. His goals were not the only talking point in the United dressing-room that day. Somebody had forgotten to pack Mark Jones' boots and they'd been left gathering dust in Manchester. Ronnie Cope had travelled with the team as reserve. With no substitutions in those days he was only going to play if someone got injured in the build-up to the game. Mark ended up playing in Ronnie's boots. They were at least three sizes too small for him and big Jonesy came off the pitch in agony.

Returning to the league, we had a crunch fixture on 18 January. It was Bolton Wanderers at Old Trafford. Manchester derby matches may be of immense significance to the red and blue halves of the city, but Bolton were an altogether more daunting prospect. They had a team nobody fancied playing. Roy Hartle, Tommy Banks and Nat Lofthouse – Wanderers didn't take any prisoners. No one slept well the night before going to Bolton, and that included Matt. For all their power, we really had their measure in that match. We took the game by the scruff of the neck and once we'd doused their fire, we started to run the show. Duncan Edwards and Albert Scanlon scored, but there was only one star of that particular show. A faired-haired youngster called Bobby Charlton scored a superb hat-trick.

A week later it was back to the Cup, and back to Old Trafford. Ipswich Town were the visitors on a muddy surface that clawed at boots and sapped stamina. Alf Ramsey was in charge of Ipswich, and my opposite number was Roy Bailey, father of Gary. Promoted from the Third Division (south) the previous season, Ipswich were an emerging side. Ted Phillips' club record 41 goals had been largely instrumental in Ipswich's rise. Ted, though, wasn't just as prolific against me. In my last game in the Second Division with Doncaster I'd saved two penalties from him, and lightning struck again as I saved Ted's spot kick in a hard-fought win.

The following Saturday we were to play Arsenal at Highbury. It was our last league match before leaving for Belgrade and our European Cup second leg. We'd beaten the Gunners 4–2 back at Old Trafford in September. Doing the double over the north Londoners would be the perfect morale booster for the trip behind the Iron Curtain. We travelled down to the Big Smoke and booked into our traditional London retreat, the Lancaster Gate Hotel. The omens didn't look good, though – our director, Mr George Whittaker, suffered a heart attack on the eve of the game. I'd got up in the middle of the night and I left my room to go to the toilet. In the corridor were two policemen and it was only later that I discovered he had died.

The game itself turned out to be a classic. We struck first, Dennis Viollet setting up Duncan, who scored with a stinging drive. I had a hand in the second goal myself. Arsenal were piling on the pressure in search of an equaliser. I plucked a cross from under my crossbar and flung it out to Albert Scanlon. Scanny's speed caught Arsenal flat-footed. The defence finally boxed him into the corner, but his perfectly flighted cross found Bobby Charlton. Bobby gave the Arsenal keeper, the great Jack Kelsey, no chance. Albert was again the architect of our third. His cross was clipped back by Kenny Morgans and Tommy Taylor headed home.

The lads were laughing and joking in the dressing-room at half-time. You could tell they thought the match was already won. Skipper Roger Byrne knew better. He offered a word of caution and he was spot on for David Herd, later to join United, pulled one back after an hour. I couldn't do much about it as the ball, and David's boot, flew past me. Before we knew what was happening they'd scored a second. When the equaliser went in, Highbury erupted. I remember the hairs on my neck standing to attention. Our pride was hurt and we bounced back. Dennis edged us back in front after brilliant interplay between Bobby and Scanny. Our fifth was sparked on the right by Kenny Morgans. He made ground down the line before slipping a peach of a pass to Tommy Taylor, who did the rest. Arsenal weren't finished and scored a fourth of their own to set up a dramatic climax to a dramatic game. One sensational comeback a game is quite enough for me and fortunately we held on for a memorable win.

It was a great time to be alive. Here I was, Harry Gregg from Windsor Avenue, a professional footballer with Manchester United. The fans on the Stretford End were indeed watching me, just as I had stood to support my old Doncaster team-mate Bill Patterson. Of the 42-strong squad, only four of us had been recruited from outside the confines of Old Trafford. I'd worked hard to get there, but being a United man was more fulfilling than I ever could have imagined. We were a group of young men with everything to play for.

III

MUNICH

The thoughts and sorrow of a nation went with the 23 men who perished in the Munich Air Disaster. By nightfall on 6 February 1958, there were few people in Britain who remained unmoved by the scale and nature of the tragedy. For most, time would be the great healer, eventually lifting the pall of gloom and returning life to some semblance of normality. For us, the ones who were there and survived, life would never be the same again.

Although we had beaten Red Star Belgrade 2–1 at Old Trafford in the first leg, none of us were under any illusions about the size of the task ahead. The Serb side were certain to come out all guns blazing and their pitch wasn't going to suit our style. With snow, slush, and surface water, conditions were so bad they'd marked the lines in red paint. It was a hostile atmosphere which greeted us at kick-off time. Red Star was the army team and everywhere you looked there were khaki-clad conscripts staring back. It was also obvious that some of the soldiers felt they were still on manoeuvres. They tried everything to break my concentration, from verbal abuse, which I could handle, to actually encroaching on to the pitch.

I might have been busy with the shenanigans going on behind my goal, but there was little to concern me on the pitch. Dennis Viollet had stuck one away early on, Bobby Charlton added two more, and with a 5–1 aggregate lead at half-time it looked all over bar the shouting. Roger Byrne wasn't falling for that one, though. He'd warned us against complacency against Arsenal a few days earlier and was right to remind us again. No sooner had the second-half started than Red Star pulled a goal back. Ten minutes later Bill Foulkes gave away a dubious penalty. They scored and all hell broke loose inside the stadium. With five minutes to go and the Yugoslavs camped in our half, I dived at one of their players' feet just on the edge of my area. As I slid across the line, Roger Byrne started frantically waving over to our bench. He thought I was injured, mistaking the red line markings I'd collected on my white shorts for blood. The Red Star crowd had reached fever pitch, yet they still managed to crank up the volume further when Kostic's free-kick deflected off Dennis Viollet and looped over my head. The final act saw the referee ignore Red Star's late penalty appeal, not an easy decision for him to make in the circumstances. We held on for a win every bit as memorable as the one at Highbury.

What a feeling! In the space of a few days we'd beaten Arsenal and Red Star Belgrade in two enthralling matches. We were unbeaten since before Christmas. In fact, we hadn't lost a game since my debut at Leicester. All was good in the United camp.

The post-match banquet was a grand affair with a replica of the Soviets' earth-orbiting satellite, Sputnik, circling the room on rails. The speeches were endless and I spotted Roger Byrne passing a note to Matt Busby. He was asking if the players could go out after the function was over. Matt looked up, puffed on his pipe, and nodded. To me it's a wonderful example of the relationship that existed between manager, captain and players. Some of the lads headed off into town, the rest of us went back to the hotel to play cards. We played poker into the wee small hours, with me betting sterling and the rest of the lads extortionate amounts of the near-worthless local currency. 'I'll see you four grand!' Boy, did they think they were high rollers. Despite the fact that I was putting in ten-shilling notes, whilst the other lads threw down Yugoslav currency and lifted mine, I still managed to skin the school. It was a great night all round, with Mark Jones, David Pegg, and Tommy Taylor belting out: 'On Ilkley Moor Baht 'at'. We also opened the suitcases full of food we'd been advised to bring from home, tucking into an eclectic, and late night, gastronomic feast which included corned beef, hard-boiled eggs and biscuits.

We left Belgrade before lunch the following day. With a fuel stop scheduled in Munich, we'd be back home in Manchester by six. On board the aircraft there were two card schools up and running. A four-handed game of hearts was in operation directly in front of me, whilst diagonally opposite Liam Whelan, Johnny Berry, Roger Byrne, Ray Wood and Jackie Blanchflower were staking a claim for top spot at poker. The card lads were giving me grief, anxious that I would take the one remaining seat and give them a chance to recoup the previous night's losses. I passed on their offer and slept throughout the flight in the two-seater just behind Bill Foulkes. I was only stirred by the chime of the 'fasten seatbelts for landing' warning bell. Munich too was gripped by winter. It wasn't as bad as Belgrade, but I recall the hundreds of footprints in the snow leading to the terminal.

Eventually our flight to Manchester was called and we filed back on board. The card players were still trying to persuade me to try my hand, but I decided to let them sweat a bit longer. I returned to my seat near the bulkhead, just in front of the *Daily Mail* photographer Peter Howard and his telegraphist Ted Ellyard. Sitting across from Ted were a lady and a baby. Across the aisle from me Bobby Charlton and David Pegg were messing about. Bobby might come across as rather dour today, but back then he was a young man with a real zest for life.

The plane taxied down the runway. I was daydreaming, gazing out of the window at the wheels below and slightly behind me. I watched the bow wave of snow and the telescopic rods extend, then, without warning, the wheels began to lock and unlock. The aircraft started to move about, went into a skid and came to a halt with a bang. The bang was white-jacketed steward Tom Cable being thrown from the galley into the empty third seat beside the woman and her baby. Visibly shaken, he strapped himself into a seat beside them. The cabin crew then explained that there had been a technical hitch. We returned to our start position and began trundling down the runway again.

The snow lay a little deeper than before. I watched as the rods extended to the point where I was sure we'd taken off. Then, just as with the first abortive take-off attempt, the brakes started locking and unlocking. This time as we ground to a halt, the aircraft slewed across the runway. The captain announced we would be returning to the terminal building. It was at this point that I recall the first seeds of doubt. There was no panic, or any real fear, it was an almost imperceptible sense that something bad was going to happen.

The minutes ticked past inside the terminal. I don't know how many. But it can't have been more than four or five judging by the surprised look on most people's faces when the tannoy announced: 'Would the United party please board the aircraft!' I climbed up the steps at the back of the aircraft and noticed that Tom Cable had this time strapped himself into the seat at the rear. He looked scared. It wasn't a good sign when the crew looked worried.

I sat directly behind Billy Foulkes. I noticed Bill's head just above the height of the seat and I thought to myself, if this thing belly-flops, his brains are going to get scrambled. I opened my shirt, tucked my collar down, then opened my trousers to get comfortable. Then I put my feet up on the frame of the seat in front. Earlier in the trip I'd been reading a book called *The Whip*, by some bloke Roger McDonald. By today's standards *The Whip* was about as raunchy as the *Beano*, but having been brought up on a diet of hellfire and brimstone, it was playing on my conscience. I thought, if anything happens here and I'm reading this it is straight to hell for me. I put the book away just before we started moving. After only a few yards, we stopped. The journalist Alf Clark was missing. He was still inside the terminal phoning his wife to say he'd be late for the Northern Sports Writers dinner. Alf finally made it on board and the lads, thinking he'd been phoning through copy, started shouting out 'Scoop! Scoop!' and dishing out a bit of stick.

We rolled away once more and I glanced diagonally across to Roger Byrne. Roger wasn't a good flyer at the best of times and he looked petrified. I thought to myself, 'He's more scared than I am', and I actually drew courage from his fear. The silence was punctuated by a nervous cough, then a snigger. Johnny Berry shouted: 'I don't know what you're laughing at. We are all going to get killed here!' Billy Whelan piped up: 'Well, if this is the time, then I'm ready.' I was later to relay those words to his family – they said it was a great source of comfort. It takes a brave man to be a coward and if only someone had said at this point 'This is crazy!' or really raised an objection, then who knows?

Bobby Charlton and David Pegg, who had been sitting across from me, got up and went to the back. Frank Taylor moved to one of their seats. This time I was glued to the window. I watched again as the wheels dispersed great waves of slush. I watched as we passed places not reached during the two previous abortive take-off attempts. And I watched as the telescopic rods fully extended and the wheels began to lift off the ground. Bang! There was a sudden crash and debris began bombarding me on all sides. One second it was light, the next dark. There were no screams, no human sounds, only the terrible tearing of metal. Sparks burst all around. I felt something go up my nose. Then something cracked my skull like a hard-boiled egg. I was hit again at the front. The salty taste of blood was in my mouth and I was terrified to put my hands up to my head.

An eerie stillness replaced the chaos, punctuated only by the interminable sound of hissing. All around was dark – it was as if I was frozen in time. Disorientated, a bulletin of random thoughts flashed through my mind. I've done well for the first time in my life . . . I won't see my little girl and wife . . . I won't see my mother and my family again . . . and I can't speak German. Then I noticed a shaft of light streaming down from just above me on the right.

I reached down to unfasten my seat belt. I hadn't even realised I was lying on my side. I started to crawl toward the light. I stuck my head through the hole and momentarily froze. Lying below me on the ground was youth team coach Bert Whalley. He was wearing an Air Force blue suit and a blue cardigan. It was Bert who had nurtured so many of the young players. He was motionless, his eyes were open and there wasn't a mark on him. Somehow, I still knew he was dead. I turned around and kicked the hole bigger. I noticed I only had one shoe, then dropped down.

For a second I thought I was the only one alive as the crackle of fire and hissing filled the air. To my left was the socket which housed one of the engines. It was burning. The rest of the wing was gone. In the distance I could see five people running away through the snow. It was the two stewardesses, the radio operator George Rogers, Peter Howard and Ted Ellyard. They shouted at me to run. Suddenly, from around the cockpit came Captain Jim Thain. He had a little fire extinguisher in his hand and when he saw me, he shouted: 'Run, you stupid bastard, it is going to explode!' It hadn't even entered my head that the fuel could soon ignite. It had to Jim Thain and his was a premeditated courage. He disappeared again around the front of the cockpit where his colleague Captain Raiment was trapped. Just then, I heard a cry. I recalled a baby in the seat just across and behind from me and I began shouting at the people running away to come back. I was angry and roared: 'Come back, you bastards, there are people alive in there.' They kept going.

I crawled back into the aircraft. Scrabbling in the darkness, I came across a child's coat. I thought of my daughter and was terrified of what I might find underneath it. There was nothing there, no baby, no seat. I heard another cry and, clambering further into the wreckage, I found the baby under a pile of debris. Unbelievably, the child only had a bad cut over one eye. I crawled out with the child and headed in the direction of the people who'd been running. George Rogers turned, came back towards me and I handed the baby to him. I told him there were more people alive. He turned and ran with the baby in his arms. I went back into the aircraft again. As I dragged myself through, a woman exploded from underneath a pile of wreckage. Lying on my backside behind her, I forced the woman along with my legs. She was in a terrible state. There was a gaping wound to her eye, and I later discovered she also had a fractured skull and two broken legs. When she eventually regained consciousness in hospital, this poor Yugoslav woman heard German voices and thought the war was still on.

I couldn't comprehend the scene of utter devastation around me. Much of the aircraft had been destroyed. One section seemed to have disappeared altogether. I found Ray Wood. He was wearing a big orange sweater. I tried, but couldn't move him. Close by was Albert Scanlon. Scanny's injuries were so severe I had to fight to prevent myself from being sick. He was also trapped and I couldn't budge him. I left thinking Ray and Albert were dead.

I began to search for Jackie Blanchflower. I shouted out his name. Blanchy and I had been friends since we played together for Ireland Schoolboys as 14-year-olds. I was desperate to find him. I stumbled across

Bobby Charlton and Dennis Viollet, hanging half in, half out of what was left of the body of the plane. Dennis had a gash behind his right ear and next to his head lay what looked like the clutch plate of a car. Again, I thought Dennis and Bobby were dead. Even so, I grabbed them by the waistbands of their trousers and trailed them through the snow for about 20 yards, away from the smouldering front of the plane.

I hadn't been around to the other side of the aircraft yet. I was stunned by what I saw. There was a house 50 or 60 yards away with half the roof torn off. Forty yards from that there was a compound with a big wire fence and a square building. Outside the building was a wagon with large fuel drums on it – and the rest of the aircraft. The plane had slid off the runway, collided with the house and cartwheeled into the building. The back section from wings to tail finished up sticking out of the petrol compound like a dart. There were explosions everywhere, sending huge plumes of flame into the sky. It was horrifying.

I found the boss. Matt was lying between what remained of the aircraft and the burning building. He was conscious. He didn't look too bad compared to what I'd seen before. He had a small cut behind his ear and was propped up on his elbows with his hands across his chest. It was what we call sitting on your kitty hunkers. He was rubbing at his chest and moaning: 'My legs, my legs.' I looked down and his foot was pointing the wrong way. I kept talking to him and propped him up with some of the wreckage. I tried to reassure him and then I left to search for Jackie. About 30 yards further on, I found him. He was crying out that he'd broken his back and was paralysed. The heat of the fires was melting the snow and he was lying in a pool of water. Thankfully, he wasn't paralysed; his inability to move was down to the fact that Roger Byrne was draped across his waist. Roger was dead. There wasn't a blemish and his eyes were open. I have always regretted that I didn't close his eyes. The front of his trousers were open and I remember thinking he must have done the same as me before take-off. Jackie told me many times after the crash that he'd just lain there watching the second hand tick by on Roger's watch.

Blanchy was still moaning. I tried to tell him he was OK, but I don't suppose I sounded very convincing. The lower part of Jackie's right arm had been almost completely severed. I took my tie off to make a tourniquet. I pulled too tight and the tie snapped. I started to frantically search for something else, scrabbling through the mud and slush. I sensed someone was there and looked up to see one of the stewardesses was staring back. I screamed at this poor shocked figure, 'Get me something to tie his arm!' All I got was that same vacant stare. I was with Jackie for quite a while, and still I had seen no one other than those directly involved in the crash. Eventually people started to come from the direction of the railway track.

I remember one guy in a tweed coat and wellington boots. He produced a hypodermic needle from a medical bag and I tried to communicate to him who I thought was dead and who I thought needed treatment. He was running from body to body and I called for him to help Jackie. It was hardly surprising that he was terrified. Every time there was an explosion he would turn and run. There was one massive blast and I watched as he was thrown into the air, landing on his arse and still holding the syringe in the air like the Statue of Liberty. More people began to appear. I looked around and Bill Foulkes was kneeling beside the boss, having made his way back. The people on the scene now were ordinary folk, not firemen or ambulance crews. Eventually one local turned up in a Volkswagen coal lorry. They put Jackie and Matt in the back, then another body, whom I only recognised from his United blazer. It was little Johnny Berry. Then, I was shocked to see Dennis Viollet and Bobby Charlton, standing staring at the fire. I couldn't believe they were alive. All of us, plus Bill Foulkes, were helped on to the truck. After a few yards we stopped, picking up Maria Miklos, wife of the courier, before heading to the Rechts der Isar Hospital. The driver went at a helluva lick, with Bill Foulkes up front berating him to slow down. He eventually resorted to punching him on the back of the head.

The hospital battled to cope with the scale of the crash. The injured and dying were being treated in the theatres, rooms, even corridors. Bill and I were asked to try to identify people as the medics attended to them. I was shocked when I was called to Ray Wood. I thought he was dead. He was in a bad way, his eye hanging out of its socket. I did my best to communicate in broken English. Finally, a group of nuns led Bill, Peter Howard, Ted Ellyard, Bobby Charlton and myself down the corridor for treatment. There was also a giant Yugoslav journalist with us. Suddenly, he slid down the wall. It turned out his legs had been broken. Heaven knows how he remained upright for so long. I was put on a trolley. They gave me an injection, but before they could treat me any further I rolled off and said I wasn't staying. Bill Foulkes followed suit. Bobby blacked out as they approached with the syringe.

Despite what I'd witnessed on the airfield it was only in that hospital that the enormity of the situation had hit home. At one stage a British diplomat appeared on the scene. He offered to get us some dry socks – not exactly our number-one priority at the time. Not when you'd listened to the hospital tannoy announce: 'Herr Swift dead!' Three words that shocked me to my core. I'd seen death, it had been all around me. Yet only when those words resonated around the corridors did the tragedy begin to register in my head. We never saw the diplomat again.

Leaving Bobby in the care of the medics, the rest of us set off for the Stathus Hotel. In an upstairs room sat Bill Foulkes, Ted Ellyard and Peter Howard, who had joined us in the hospital after phoning his newspaper from the airport's terminal building. I stood at the window for what seemed like an eternity. Bewildered by what had just happened, I stared as the cars in the street below gradually disappeared under a blanket of snow.

IV

SAVING MY SANITY

I didn't get much sleep in the Stathus Hotel that night. Most of the time I just resided in a sort of personal purgatory, a no man's land between awake and asleep. Now and again the silence was shattered by the tormented shouts from the bed next to me. I was rooming with Bill Foulkes and through the night he struggled with his subconscious, haunted no doubt by thoughts and images of the crash a few hours earlier. It was one of the longest nights of my life.

Jimmy Murphy travelled out to Munich to escort the two of us home. It was a journey which also took us to hell and back. On that tortuous rail trek via the Hook of Holland we were constantly reminded of the crash. Every time the train's brakes were applied, the sights and sounds of the aircraft slewing all over that slush-covered runway came racing back. Jimmy did his best to lift our spirits. At one point a Chinese man came into our compartment and Jimmy said: 'All right, me old china, any of your sons play football?' It would have been a funny moment under any other circumstances. I also met the actor Rupert Gregg who said he was sorry about the accident. I was in such a state that I couldn't even muster a reply. Jimmy hired a taxi for the final leg back to Manchester and the families we thought we might never see again.

Jimmy was a tower of strength. Not only in the way he'd guided us home, but also in setting aside his personal grief to assemble a side for our postponed FA Cup fifth-round tie with Sheffield Wednesday. Although it wasn't something I gave any consideration too, speculation was that we wouldn't be able to field a team, but that was not the attitude instilled at

Old Trafford by Matt and Jimmy. Playing again, and soon, was just what I needed. It saved my sanity. I couldn't get to the ground quick enough for training. Those brief moments spent running, diving, kicking, arguing and fighting were my escape valve.

Thirteen days after the crash and swept along by a tidal wave of emotion, we played Sheffield Wednesday at Old Trafford in front of 59,848 people. Thousands more stood silently outside the stadium. Of the Busby Babes who beat Red Star Belgrade, only two, Bill Foulkes and myself, walked down the tunnel.

They tell me you could almost reach out and touch the goodwill that cascaded down from the terraces. They wanted to help, to play their part, and it worked. Shay 'Bomber' Brennan with two, and Alex Dawson were our scorers. I was almost oblivious to the poignancy of the game, a numbness taking hold. I had no real feeling of elation. I do recall, though, sitting in the dressing-room after the match. It was there that a sense of a job well done gave way to thoughts of the tragedy less than two weeks before. Suddenly, the desire to play football, the energy I somehow found in my race to escape the anguish, all but evaporated. I felt tired. All I wanted to do now was go home and be with my family.

The supporters had carried this team of largely unfamiliar faces on to victory. The banner headline in the programme that night read: 'United will go on'. It also contained some poignant words penned by our chairman, Harold Hardman. It concluded: 'Although we mourn the dead and grieve for our wounded, we believe that great days are not done for us. The sympathy and encouragement of the football world, and particularly our supporters, will justify and inspire us. The road back may be long and hard, but with the memory of those who died at Munich, of their stirring achievements and wonderful sportsmanship ever with us, Manchester United will rise again.'

I was playing my part too, but only just. Not only was I trying to cope with the maelstrom of emotions raging inside my head, but also physical pain from undiagnosed injuries.

Eventually, the headaches would get so bad that I needed to use my tie, which I twisted around my head in bed at night, as a makeshift tourniquet.

I remember one game where I had to hold on to the sides of the tunnel before running out. Eventually I was taking phenobarbitone, a drug used to induce sleep, which a friend of Bill Foulkes called Norman Brierley had been prescribed after a bad car accident. He passed on those little pills to me. Finally, I asked to see a neurosurgeon. He told me I had a fractured skull.

Back at training I was keeping myself occupied, particularly with two new players, Stan Crowther and Ernie Taylor, drafted in. There was a style to our play which required some understanding. The Busby Babes knew this; new men had to be assimilated. Time was of the essence on this occasion. I'm not being deliberately disrespectful, but necessity meant that players arrived at United who, in other circumstances, wouldn't have made the cut. Some couldn't cope with life at Old Trafford, others, like Mark Pearson, looked to the manor born. Jimmy Murphy loved Mark. With his trendy haircut and long sideburns, plus a broken nose courtesy of a kicking he received at Belle-Vue, the 'teddy boy' tag didn't take long to stick. Ironically, it had been teddy boys who'd broken his nose. His appearance may have suggested 'wide boy', but he wasn't like that in any way. Two others who gelled effectively were Alex Dawson, a young man built like a brick outhouse, and Shay Brennan, who would eventually become a close friend.

It was a time of rapid transition and I felt a certain responsibility to help in any way I could. It wasn't a great time to be advising others, however, because I was busy questioning myself. I was always supremely self-assured when it came to my goalkeeping, not arrogant, just confident enough to cope with all that being a Manchester United player entailed. There was one game, though, when I was uncomfortable about my performance. I stayed on at the training ground, hoping to iron out any flaws. I was on my own throwing the ball about when Jimmy Murphy came over and asked what I was doing. I confessed my concerns and Jimmy stared at me with this fierce gaze. He said he'd tell me when I needed extra training. He told me to go home and I instantly felt like a million dollars. It was a great act of man management, typical of Jimmy and Matt. Jimmy, in particular, had an instinctive knack of knowing just what to say. It is why the wee Welshman was so invaluable to the club.

We had beaten Sheffield Wednesday in the cup, but any lift it provided was soon dashed. Two days after the game I was enjoying a bit of a lie-in. When I eventually surfaced I hunted in vain for the morning papers we always had delivered. They had been hidden, and I was soon to find out why. Across its front page was the news that Duncan Edwards had died in Munich. It devastated me. It wasn't that Duncan meant more to me than any of the others who had lost their lives, it was just that he had been alive when I'd left Munich. We'd gone into the ward to see the lads before heading home. I walked with the Chief Surgeon, Professor Georg Maurer, as he did his rounds, stopping at each bed to give his prognosis. He said Jackie and Scanny would be OK, that Matt was a strong man and that Duncan was a strong boy. We then went over to where Johnny Berry was lying with wires and tubes protruding all over the place. He looked at Johnny and said: 'I am not God.'

During our last visit Duncan had briefly come round, asking Jimmy Murphy what time kick-off was. With his eyes welling up, Jimmy told him: 'Three o'clock, son.' Duncan said: 'Get stuck in!' then lapsed back into a state of unconsciousness. He was such a strong lad it just never entered my head that he might not make it. Duncan's death somehow brought the horror of the tragedy in Germany sharply into focus once more. I cried for the first time since the crash. It would be many years later, and under the full glare of the television cameras, before I would break down again about Munich.

Football again was my salvation. We were drawn against West Bromwich Albion in the sixth round of the FA Cup and, after a 2–2 draw, we brought them back to Old Trafford. The Midlanders, who were a tasty side, had Don Howe at right-back and Bobby Robson at wing-half. They'd already beaten us 4–3 earlier in the season on our patch, and there was even more interest than usual in the outcome of the replay when West Brom's manager, Vic Buckingham, said his side would not be lulled into feeling sorry for us. He announced they'd win 6–0. We weren't looking for anyone's pity, we just wanted to win. And win we did, with Bobby Charlton playing in his first game since Munich. It was a brilliant run by Bobby which supplied the ammunition for Colin Webster to score the only goal of the game.

The semi-final with Fulham also went to a replay, this time at neutral Highbury. It was a poignant moment for me when I ran out for that match in the stadium where the Busby Babes had turned it on against Arsenal in our last game before Belgrade. We'd won 5–4 then, and again we scored five. Alex Dawson hit a hat trick, with Bobby Charlton and Shay Brennan weighing in with one each. It finished 5–3 and amazingly this patched-up club was heading for Wembley.

Jimmy took us all off to Blackpool's Norbreck Hydro Hotel to recharge our batteries, a blast along the beach on mopeds proving to be one of the lighter moments since the crash. With so many replays the games had been coming thick and fast and in hindsight that break probably did us no good. We definitely lost some of our momentum, and for those of us who survived Munich, there was now too much time to dwell on matters. I'd be lying, though, if I said we weren't ready for the final with Bolton Wanderers. The mood was determined – we'd come this far, we weren't about to lose now. However, whatever had taken us this far, emotion, luck, I don't know, it ran out beneath the Twin Towers.

At Wembley I was more conscious than perhaps anywhere else of the toll taken by Munich. I'd played there for Northern Ireland against England just prior to joining United. Our centre-half was United's Jackie Blanchflower; his immediate opponent was Tommy Taylor. Also in the England side were Roger Byrne and Duncan Edwards. Now Jackie's career was finished, and Tommy, Roger and Duncan were dead. And if you think the footballing gods would take our loss into account, well, you can think again. We had luck alright, but it was all bad. It manifested itself in the shape of Bolton's Nat Lofthouse. Nat barged me, and the ball, into the net for his side's decisive second goal. Ten times out of ten today it would merit a free kick. Sadly, not in 1958. Nat admitted after the match that it had been a foul. It did little to alleviate my sense of injustice. I swore to get my revenge.

Nat and I are good friends, but when he announced the following season that he planned to retire, I got down on my knees at night to pray he would be around long enough for me to give him a whack. Nat retired, then was lured back. His comeback game? Yes, you've guessed it,

Manchester United at Old Trafford. I plotted just how my thinly veiled assault would take place. And early on I thought my chance had arrived. I came for a ball, grabbed it and kept my head down. I could see Nat approaching out of the corner of my eye, but he turned away and the opportunity was gone.

A year later and my fixation with Nat was still festering. This time we were at Bolton. Nat was being partnered up front by an international colleague of mine, Billy McAdams. Not long after the start I collected one high ball off Nat's head and when we both landed I grabbed his ankle and tried to twist his bloody leg off. He screamed – I let go. Then, in the second-half, I again came for a high ball. I caught a glimpse of a white shirt and hit it with everything I had. The game was stopped and there was Billy lying in a heap with a busted face. Seeing my Northern Ireland team-mate and friend in a crumpled mess on the ground, I vowed to draw a line under my personal vendetta with the Lion of Vienna. Many years later I appeared for Nat on *This Is Your Life*. I stood behind a screen and told everyone he was a dirty so and so and that if he tried the same thing again he'd be done for GBH. Nat turned and shouted: 'Greggy!' There are no hard feelings between us. I respect him immensely as a footballer and a man.

There would be no winners' medal from the cup, but at least we didn't have time to dwell on it. AC Milan were due at Old Trafford in the first leg of the European Cup semi-final. When Jimmy Murphy had been putting together a makeshift team for the FA Cup match with Sheffield Wednesday, the authorities had given special dispensation for Stan Crowther to play – he'd already played in the competition for Aston Villa. Now, the FA were returning to type. The suits refused to allow Bobby Charlton to play against the Italians because he was needed for a meaningless international friendly with Portugal. Ernie Taylor took Bobby's place. We won 2–1, Dennis Viollet scoring the first and winning the vital penalty which Taylor converted to give us a slender first-leg lead. The FA Cup final had been Dennis' first game back since the crash and in the last few minutes of the Milan game he was bearing down on goal. In his path was Cesare Maldini, father of current Milan skipper Paolo.

Maldini body-checked Dennis and Danish referee Helge pointed to the spot. Maldini, in typical Italian style, collapsed on the pitch, beside himself with grief. Tough, that's what I say. His was the classic professional foul and we gratefully accepted that goal advantage for the trip to north Italy.

As it turned out, Ernie Taylor's penalty was irrelevant. Milan stuffed us 4–0 in the return leg. They outplayed us, although they did also have an extra man in the shape of the German referee Albert Deutsch. Herr Deutsch was not strong enough to cope with the raucous atmosphere and the antics of the Milan bench, who on four occasions actually invaded the pitch to contest a decision.

The season was over. Gone was the emotional crutch which had carried me through since Munich. I'd thrown everything into football, and yet, when the final whistle blew, I found that I could carry on. For all of us who were involved in the crash, the ghosts of 6 February would never be truly exorcised. But at least I'd proved to myself that Harry Gregg was alive and kicking.

V

PAYING THE PRICE

Matt Busby returned home a month after the Munich Air Disaster. To this day the only people who knew I went to see him shortly afterwards are Matt's wife Jean, his son Sandy and daughter Sheena. We talked at length about Germany, about everything except the crash itself. He spoke of the pain, about how his lungs were in such a poor state that they couldn't administer anaesthetic when they reset his shattered foot a bone at a time. But it was not the physical pain which troubled him most. The mental scars ran much deeper.

Matt told me about Johnny Berry after he regained consciousness. Digger would come into Matt's room and talk about the players. On one occasion Johnny said: 'That bloody Tommy Taylor, some friend he is. He hasn't even been to see me.' Matt hadn't the heart to tell him Tommy was dead. This went on for days, until Matt finally snapped. Johnny, who'd suffered severe head injuries, was going on about how he hadn't got much sleep the night before because Tommy Steele was playing guitar in his room. Matt found himself barking back: 'Tommy Steele's in South Africa!'

Part of me wanted to confess to Matt all that I had suffered, and was suffering, but I thought it unfair to heap yet more misery on a man who now looked considerably older than his 48 years. Mental torment, that was the real legacy of Munich. For those who survived, and those who lost loved ones, it was a constant battle against grief, guilt and, eventually in many cases, bitterness.

Johnny Berry wanted nothing more than to be allowed to return to training with us. But, even that was asking too much. The brain injury he'd sustained left him so vulnerable that any blow to the head was potentially fatal. Johnny soon felt totally alienated. For someone so vibrant, being permanently consigned to the sidelines was a living hell. He was not a quitter, but that's exactly what they were asking him to do. Eventually Johnny and his wife Hilda became extremely bitter.

With hindsight you can see that Manchester United's administration had been decimated by the crash, but Johnny and Hilda viewed the lack of support from the club as lack of interest. The situation wasn't helped when officials called, as they also did with Jackie Blanchflower, to say that the club house they lived in had to be vacated. Less than 12 months after his career was prematurely curtailed on that runway in Munich, Jackie was on the dole and looking for a place to live. As the years passed resentment grew. When Johnny Berry died the old guard in Manchester phoned me in Ireland to ask would I speak to Hilda. John Doherty from the Manchester United Old Boys' Association wanted to send a wreath of red and white carnations as tribute, but felt unsure if it was the right thing to do. Hilda was more than happy to give her blessing, but it still gives you an indication of just how deep the ill-feeling ran.

Kenny Morgan's is another case in point. Prior to the crash Kenny was going through a purple patch which saw him displace Johnny Berry. Two-footed, with pace to burn, it looked as though a bright future lay ahead for the teenager. Kenny returned to action a few months after Munich and looked all set to play in the Cup final against Bolton. Kenny maintains that Jimmy Murphy came to him on the Friday and told him he was in the starting line-up. Then, as the team was walking around Wembley the following morning, Jimmy went over and told him Matt had decided to go with Dennis Viollet instead. It broke Kenny. He seemed to lose a couple of yards of pace after that and by 1961 had moved on to Swansea. Kenny claims Matt and Jimmy promised they would look after him if he made the move to his native Wales, but in reality it was out of sight, out of mind.

Each family has its story. Few are more poignant than that of the Bents. Geoff Bent's wife Marion had just given birth to their first child and Dad made it clear he didn't want to leave mother and baby's side. Marion persuaded him to go to Belgrade and she blamed herself for his death. The truth is that Geoff Bent wasn't even scheduled to travel. The original plan was that Ronnie Cope would travel to Belgrade, not Geoff. Then against Arsenal Roger Byrne picked up a slight knock and Matt decided to take Geoff as cover. Consequently, Ronnie missed the trip. He was fuming and planned to hand in a transfer request on the team's return. Little did Ronnie know that being dropped from the squad could well have saved his life. Ronnie stayed on at Old Trafford after the crash, stepping into the breach left by the death of Mark Jones and Jackie Blanchflower's enforced retirement.

Albert Scanlon continued his career after the crash, but he too feels a certain sense of injustice. A local lad, Scanny was one of the game's great characters. When we went on foreign trips, he would always be out and about in town with a seemingly endless array of local contacts. Everyone appeared to know *our* Albert. No sooner had we arrived at our chosen destination than he would be pulling on his trademark white raincoat and heading off. I was rooming with him on one trip and I was determined to find out what he was up to. So, after dinner, Joe Friday (the name we gave him after the television detective who wore the same style coat) left and I followed. I found him in our room thumbing through the telephone directory. I asked who he was phoning and he said he didn't know yet. As it turned out, there was method to Scanny's madness. When he arrived on foreign shores he would look through the phone book until he found an English name. There was a fair chance he was an ex-pat, so Scanny would ring the person up and ask if they fancied a night out. One phone call, one night out, one ready-made tour guide.

Albert's grievances stem from his return to Piccadilly Station following the crash. Waiting for him was a black taxi and Scanny, still on crutches, hobbled over and got in. The cabbie told him it was his until such times as he didn't need it any more, a show of solidarity from Manchester's taxi fraternity. On the day of the FA Cup semi-final with Fulham at Villa Park, Albert was approached in the car park by United's Secretary Les Olive. He stopped Albert and told him it was time to give up the taxi, the club couldn't justify paying for it any more. Les had assumed the club were footing the bill. Albert set him straight, although the incident did little to endear the club to a man whom I've always found to be a giver, not a taker.

At the time of the Munich Memorial match he said there were two things he wanted to do if he got a few quid. One was to send money to the family of the steward killed outside Coventry's ground. The other, to send a donation to the Omagh Bomb Fund.

It would have been perfectly natural to assume that Manchester United would step forward to cosset and protect after Munich. The fact that they didn't, however, was not a deliberate act of negligence. The truth of the matter was that there was no one around who could help. Matt was in hospital and the crash had claimed the lives of Tom Curry, our trainer, Bert Whalley, youth-team coach, and the dominant figure that was Walter Crickmer. Walter, who had been caretaker manager before Matt Busby took over, had been secretary and hub of the club's administration. Les Olive took over as secretary. He was a former player who had failed to make the grade and pre-crash was nothing more than an office boy. As for the Board, it consisted of an ageing chairman, Harold Hardman, Alan Gibson, whose father had saved Manchester United from going out of business in 1932, and Bill Young.

With the club's administration in chaos, the onus fell on the Professional Footballers Association – particularly with regard to compensation. I have to point out, though, that money was never an issue with Matt Busby and the players. We had enough to contend with coming to terms with the horrors of the crash and the loss of friends and teammates. For others, though, the question of compensation was of paramount importance. In the corridors of power at Old Trafford questions were being asked about who would be held accountable; the Munich airport authorities were sweating, and at British European Airways, whose flight it was, they were really biting their nails. These people only wanted to know two things – who would have to pay, and how much? It would eventually become downright petty.

The PFA's representative, Cliff Lloyd, advised us to go to the Manchester legal firm of George Davis. He informed us that BEA were willing to look at a claim for lost baggage. They worked out that my claim would be exactly £97. Later I was called in to see our solicitor. He presented me with a letter outlining BEA's policy to pay in round figures and the enclosed cheque for

£100. More than a year later and BEA was getting increasingly annoyed at comments made in the newspapers by survivors. They decided to consider claims for physical and mental damage and I was advised to request £750. Eventually, the money arrived, again with an accompanying letter. It stated: 'Please advise your client Mr Gregg that he was overpaid by £3 on his previous claim for cabin luggage. Hence, find enclosed a cheue for £747.' I immediately took the money to Reuben Kaye. A leading accountant, United fanatic (he had a huge painting of Duncan Edwards hanging above his office desk) and close friend, Reuben was someone I trusted implicitly.

The chaotic nature of things at Old Trafford in 1958 may justify the lack of support. What it doesn't do is explain the next four decades. Many fans rightly feel embarrassed by the lack of a discernible contribution by the club to the survivors and relatives of those who lost their lives. Louis and Martin Edwards in particular, have consistently refused to accept any responsibility. They came along after the event, clearly felt no part of it, and only paid lip service to the crash when convenient. It's been okay to have the name of Dennis Viollet or Harry Gregg emblazoned across the back of retro replica shirts in the club's superstore, but heaven forbid United would actually dip into its own coffers. Anything that has been done, like the Munich memorial match for example, was nothing more than a public relations exercise in which Joe Public paid.

I know there are some who feel that Matt Busby could, and perhaps should, have forced the club's hand in the years after Munich. There's no doubt that he was a powerful figure at Old Trafford, but there was also an inherent deference to authority which held him back. Coming from a working-class mining community, Matt, as manager, director, or knight of the realm, didn't feel it was his place to dictate what should be done. The boss carried a lot of guilt from 6 February 1958, until the day he died, and I can't begin to contemplate how tough it must have been. He was the one who led United on that European adventure, and no one felt the loss of the young men nurtured at Old Trafford more than he. I do know that in his later years Matt admitted his regret at not doing more. He once said as much in an interview with a television station, then asked for that answer to be axed from the programme.

United's intransigence has been a source of great disappointment to me. But what has probably rankled most is the lies told about the crash by people who were actually there. I have no grudge against those who ran away from the crash scene at Munich. Maybe, on another day, I might have been running alongside. What I cannot forgive is the rewriting of events. Even today there is an ex-player whose CV states that injury prevented him from travelling to Belgrade. A regular on the after-dinner circuit, he's lived off that since, which disgusts me. The player in question had appeared for the first team, yes, but he was never going to Yugoslavia. In fact, even after the crash he didn't make the starting line-up. It wasn't until the following season that he made any real breakthrough. And when Manchester United played Bayern Munich in the Champions League there was a German who spoke about how he had been a fireman and that the plane had come to halt at a mound of earth. Strange, I don't remember any mound of earth, or any fireman. I don't live with Munich every day, but I cannot stomach such blatant untruths. Frank Taylor's book *When A Team Died* is also a case in point. Frank wrote about the efficiency of the German authorities, about a fleet of ambulances and fire crews following the plane down the runway on that final abortive take-off attempt. If that was true, then why the hell did we travel to the hospital in the back of a Volkswagen coal van? I rang Frank and asked just how far you could take poetic licence. Subsequent journalistic investigations back up my version of events. Ricky Kelehar, who produced a documentary on the Babes for Granada Television, found out that the emergency services' response consisted of a solitary fireman who actually went to the wrong side of the airfield. How can you compliment the airport authorities when their actions clearly don't merit it? I mean, when the firemen eventually arrived they were told to cover the bodies with car covers from the VIP parking area. The same man who gave that order also insisted they return to the mortuary to retrieve the covers and place them back on the cars.

There was also John Roberts' book *The Team That Would Not Die*, which was serialised in the *Daily Express* over the course of a week. I was staggered by what I read. The event he was describing couldn't have been the same one I survived, so I bought the book. After reading it cover to cover I phoned

John Roberts. I made it clear I had no intention of going public, but I had to tell him it was the biggest load of fiction I'd ever read. I also pointed out that he'd quoted me, yet we'd never spoken. His excuse was that he hadn't been able to trace me, not the most difficult thing to do when I was a member of a very exclusive club. I was one of only 92 people at the time managing English football league clubs. I quizzed him on where he got his background and he confessed the bulk of the detail originated with Bill Foulkes.

I found it impossible to ignore this tinkering with the truth and, in search of some advice and perhaps some form of corroboration, I placed a call to Matt Busby asking to come and see him. Jean made us both a cup of tea, then left us in peace. I told him about the book. I added that nobody owed me anything, but I just wanted to tell him the true story of what happened. He puffed away on his pipe in the living room of his King's Road home in Chorlton whilst I talked him through my Munich experiences step by painful step. I also confessed my anger at the twisting of the truth by others. When I'd finished, Matt said: 'A man must do, what a man must do.'

I had always adopted a policy of non-confrontation with Bill Foulkes. However, a chance encounter at The Cliff left me with no option but to let him know what I thought. I was at the training ground shooting the breeze with Theresa (the cook), Billy Watts, groundsman Dave Royle and the rest of the canteen staff. Bill walked in and said good morning. At this stage I had no intention of broaching the subject, nor did I plan to make idle chit chat with him. So, rather than make everyone feel awkward I politely said hello, picked up my coffee and walked off to the staff room. Seconds later the door burst open and Bill stormed in. He began to accuse me of repeatedly embarrassing him and being obstructive. I enquired if he wanted to know why. Then, I asked him to shut the door and give us some privacy. I told him that I was sure he wanted his family to be proud of him, as I did mine, but he'd been living a lie for 17 years. I told him he was a long way from the aircraft, not as he said walking around at one end. He'd also spoken of seeing me with a baby in my arms when the truth is he'd been heading in the other direction.

Authors and journalists have been chronicling the crash annually since 1958. During one interview I gave to Max Arthur I suggested that if I ever won the pools I would like to reunite the Munich survivors. It was a throwaway line, but a few years later during my stint as manager of Swansea City I received an out of the blue phone call from Max. He was very excited and told me my dream (which, incidentally, had now become his idea) was about to become reality. Knowing that Ray Wood was in the Middle East, and both Bill Foulkes and Dennis Viollet in America, I asked who was paying. Max informed me that the *Daily Express* had secured exclusive rights to photograph the survivors. Tom Lawrence, Sports Editor of the *Express*, had made the arrangements. I asked where this grand reunion was to be held and was shocked when Max said Old Trafford. He explained that Jim Barker, the restaurant manager, had agreed to give us a special rate for the meal. I could have punched a hole in the wall. They wanted the nine survivors to get together at Old Trafford, present the club with a priceless piece of PR and then pay for the privilege. Max said the *Express* was paying, but it wasn't about the money, it was the principle. I told him I wouldn't be going. I phoned Tom Lawrence to discuss the matter and the venue was switched to the Midland Hotel, the traditional base for club banquets. I then called Johnny Berry and spoke to his wife Hilda. Before she went to tell him I was on the line, Hilda warned that if I tried to persuade Digger to go I would never speak to him again.

I travelled from Swansea to my home in Manchester the evening before the reunion. When I got there Carolyn showed me a copy of the Manchester *Evening News*. The banner headline read: 'The First Get Together Of The Munich Survivors'. Accompanying the article was a picture of Martin Edwards. The story said he would be representing the club at the function. Representing the club – what the hell were we doing? I rang Mike Dempsey (Northern Sports Editor of the *Express*) and told him I wouldn't be going. At close to midnight he called me back. He'd spoken to Martin Edwards, who would now not be attending, and asked did I mind if Les Olive came along. I told Mike that Les had more right to be there than me.

Eight of us gathered in the Midland Hotel. We laughed and joked, revelling in each other's company. Albert Scanlon confessed to Jimmy Murphy he'd been terrified of him. Jimmy told Scanny he should still be.

Later in the evening someone mentioned there was a function at Old Trafford. A few of the lads wanted to go. I gave my reasons for giving it a miss and Dennis Viollet accused me of being my usual awkward self. There was no way I was darkening Old Trafford's door that night, but I did follow Jackie Blanchflower to ensure he got there safely. Jackie was a bit the worse for wear and I later found out he'd run across Martin Edwards. Now Jackie was not a man to use profanity, but that night he left Martin in no doubt as to just what he thought of his father, Louis.

The survivors met up again in 1998 thanks to a moving invite from UEFA to attend the Champions League final in Munich. The letter, which I have to admit brought a lump to my throat, said that without us the European Cup would not enjoy the prestige it does today. A press conference was arranged for after our arrival in Germany and the seven of us (Johnny Berry had sadly passed away) sat around a table to answer questions from the world's media. Bill Foulkes spoke first, repeating the nonsense about travelling to hospital in an ambulance. I was sitting at the other end of the table and I interrupted: 'Excuse me, don't you mean a coal van?'

I know the passage of time can play tricks on the mind, but there's no way I could sit back and listen to a further distortion of the truth. The problem is that if told often enough, supposition and hearsay can be translated into fact. I can understand, if not entirely forgive, fuzzy nostalgia. But it is vital that the truth doesn't become buried. We owe it to the memory of those left behind on that runway to tell it like it was.

Each of us reacted differently to the crash, and to its aftermath. On the one hand I somehow found the courage to climb back into that burning wreckage; yet it also took me four decades to summon up the courage to speak to Joy Byrne, Marion Bent, David Pegg's family and many others. It was classic survivor's guilt. I couldn't look these people in the eye knowing I'd lived when their loved ones perished. I had actually stayed with Roger and Joy Byrne a week before the crash. I was still living in Doncaster and travelling to and from Yorkshire was hardly ideal. The Byrnes kindly put me up and I befriended their little dog, or rather it befriended me. My new canine companion spent the night in my room and to my horror I found the next morning that it had used the bedroom floor as a toilet. I didn't know it at the time but Roger and Joy were in stitches as they peeked through the door the next morning to watch me scrubbing away at the floor.

It wasn't until 1998 that I finally confronted my demons. Even then, it took one of my daughters to force the issue. This cathartic process began with the Munich Memorial Service at Manchester Cathedral. I was sitting in my pew when four people moved into the row in front. One of them, a man in his forties, turned around and asked could he shake my hand. I was completely taken by surprise when he introduced himself: 'My name is Roger Byrne.' I knew before I even glanced over that Joy, who was unaware she was pregnant when her husband flew to Yugoslavia, would be sitting close by. Even then, I couldn't bring myself to initiate a meeting. I didn't have long to wait, though. It would take place 24-hours later, on the evening of the match with Bolton Wanderers.

It was my daughter Jane who helped lift a cloud which had hung over me for nearly four decades. At the post-match function Jane went across to Joy Byrne, forcing me to follow suit. Joy looked at me and said: 'Harry Gregg, why have you been torturing yourself for 40 years?'

That night washed away years of guilt. Joy's compassion seemed to open the floodgates and I also spoke to David Pegg's mother, sister and brother-in-law. I flitted from here to there, until finally I stepped outside the banqueting hall for a breath of fresh air. Standing outside was Marion Bent. She was with her daughter, who explained that Marion didn't feel she had the right to be in there. I took Marion in, escorted her to the wives' table, and introduced her to people she'd once been close to – Teresa Foulkes, Barbara Viollet, Molly Leach (Duncan Edwards' fiancée) and one lady who said: 'I bet you don't know me, Harry Gregg?' I did, it was Barbara Kershaw, first wife of Duncan's best friend Jimmy Payne.

Marion Bent is one of the real heroes of Munich. I know that every anniversary the names of Bobby Charlton, Harry Gregg, Bill Foulkes and Duncan Edwards are always mentioned, but what of the others who have suffered in silence. What about the families of men like Willie Satinoff? It's as if the loss of their loved ones is somehow less important. Willie Satinoff was head of a family business which manufactured Alligator Rainwear. I remember him as a quiet, unassuming man whom we were led to believe would soon be joining the Manchester United Board. I spoke to his family at their factory not long after the crash. I met them again in 1998 at the memorial service. A young man, I don't know if he was a grandchild, asked me what Willie was like. He told me that this function was the first contact the club had with the Satinoff family since 1958.

The loss of so many Busby Babes was a tragedy for football. But little mention is ever given to the catastrophic cull that afflicted journalism. There was Alf Clark, a complete United fanatic and footie writer with the Manchester *Evening News*. Alf had been around Old Trafford so long he'd given up on the pretence of impartiality and spoke of *we*. It was hard to imagine the press box without him. Tom Jackson, a barrel of a man who loved a bit of craic; Don Davies, a throwback to the old school who worked under the pseudonym Old International; Archie Ledbrook, Leddy to most; the *Daily Mail*'s Eric Thompson; George Follows of the *Daily Herald*; Frank Swift, an idol of mine during his playing career; and the irrepressible Henry Rose. In all, eight sportswriters perished at Munich. These were men whom you could respect. They entertained and informed, unlike some of today's salacious scandal mongers. The journalists, the flight crew, the passengers – these people are the forgotten souls of Munich. They are the people whose memory is insulted by those who have felt the need to attach themselves to the crash, to jump on the Munich bandwagon.

No one, though, was more harshly treated by the events of 6 February than Captain James Thain. He may have survived the crash, but much of what he lived for was taken away that day. He was made a scapegoat and the evidence which would have cleared his name was suppressed by his own government. I spoke to Jim Thain back in the hotel on the night of the crash. He explained the procedures for take-off and, with the events still harrowingly fresh in his mind, told me it was the drag factor which caused the crash. In the decade after the crash there were two official inquiries by the Germans and two by the British. The Germans maintained ice on the wings was to blame; the British said it was slush on the runway. Sadly, for Jim Thain, a secret meeting of ministers in April

1969 decided that diplomatic relations with Germany were more important than clearing his name. Declassified papers, which only came to light in August 2001, show Lord Chalfont, the Foreign Minister, warning that to ask the Germans to hold another inquiry: '. . . would only lose us German goodwill'.

I met Jim Thain again ten years later. I had just been appointed manager of Shrewsbury Town and the club's chairman, Tim Yates, was giving me a guided tour of Gay Meadow. He mentioned that we had a mutual friend. It turned out to be Jim (they had flown together during the Second World War). Later in the season when we played Reading I had lunch with Jim, his wife and daughter. Captain Thain maintained his innocence until his death in 1975. His own government agreed, yet they let a man, and his family, suffer the indignity of being blamed for one of the blackest days in British football. Jim Thain has been a convenient scapegoat for far too long. It's time the real culprits, the men in the shadows, were finally dragged out to face the consequences. Just don't hold your breath.

In contrast to Jim Thain, I was dubbed 'The Hero Of Munich'. It's a tag I've never felt comfortable with. For the media, though, there was a real fascination with the story of how I'd saved a Yugoslav woman and her child from the crash. And, of course, a reunion would make great television. Most of the people on board the aircraft knew Mrs Lukic. She was the wife of Yugoslavia's Air Attaché, a man who'd been second-in-command to Marshall Tito during the Second World War. In the years after the crash I'd often thought about Verena. I remembered her terrible injuries and how in hospital, when she heard the nuns talking German, she'd thought the war had broken out again. To be honest, I wondered just how she'd survived.

It was during my time as manager of Crewe Alexandra that a television company phoned about Munich. The woman's name was Joanna Cash and she asked would I meet with the child that I'd saved, now an English teacher in Belgrade. They were flying her to England and wanted me to take part in the show. I discussed things with my wife and decided I'd love to meet Vesna, provided it was in the privacy of my own home. Next morning Joanna Cash rang for an answer and I explained my reasoning. She accused me of being a coward and ranted and raved about the amount of red tape involved in bringing Vesna over, and the expense. I enquired as to how Vesna's mother was, adding that red tape would not have been a problem, citing the close connection to Marshal Tito. Within a week there was a story in the *Pink* with the headline: 'Munich Hero Snubs The Child He Saved'.

Vesna, Verena and I did meet a few years later. Stan Liversedge, who was my ghost writer when I had a column in the *People*, asked would I consider meeting the mother and daughter on a programme to be hosted by Ian St John. Ian was making the breakthrough into television and I agreed. As the date of the reunion grew closer I became extremely apprehensive. I just didn't know how I'd react. Verena and Vesna flew into Manchester and were taken to meet my family. It was big news and Carolyn phoned me in Wales to tell me that reporters were actually fighting in our front room. I advised her to call the police. Eventually, my meeting with the Lukics' took place in Phil Boersma's house in Swansea (where I was coach). I sat nervously in one of the rooms and then Vesna and Verena were brought in. It was all too much. I broke down and cried for the first time since hearing of the news of Duncan Edwards' death. Not long afterwards I received a letter from a war veteran who said he'd been so touched that he himself had cried for the first time since the war. Vesna translated for her mum, who was at pains to point out that I'd actually saved three lives. It turned out Verena had been pregnant and, despite her injuries, had given birth to a son, Dragan.

Over the years I've kept in touch with the Lukics, or to be more accurate, my wife and family did. When the Balkan conflict was at its height, Carolyn received a phone call from Vesna. She was in Israel and was in a state about her brother back home who ran the risk of being shot. She said the only country he could get into without a visa was the Republic of Ireland. She was wondering could I help. In the end what could have been an extremely awkward situation resolved itself. Her brother escaped.

For those people who directly suffered at Munich – the survivors and the families left bereaved – the issue of reparation raised its head again when a fund-raising match was proposed. However, in my eyes that match was just another huge publicity stunt by the club. It might have looked altruistic, but let's face it, it was the punters pushing their way through the turnstiles who were quite literally paying. In the end though, I had little option but to attend. I'd been to watch an Irish League match and listened as spectators discussed a bomb blast in Omagh. When I reached home I asked my wife if she'd heard anything about it. Carolyn confirmed the tragic news from Omagh, then said she had more bad news. Jean Blanchflower had phoned – Jackie was dying. Blanchy and I had been friends for more than 50 years and it wasn't until the following day that I felt composed enough to ring back. I spoke to Jean, and then to Jackie. He asked was I going to the Memorial match and, as Blanchy seldom darkened Old Trafford's door, I sensed he desperately wanted to attend. There was no way I was going to allow him to travel on his own.

I was halfway down the M6 when I finally managed to speak to United's Secretary Ken Ramsden. I told him I'd call him back from the next service station. I broke the news that Blanchy was terminally ill and asked Ken to ensure there would be a car laid on to collect him and his family. Two of my daughters, Karen and Suzanne, and my son John accompanied me to the match.

There's no doubt that the Munich Air Crash has had a profound effect on my life. And yet, harrowing and tragic as it was, Munich was not the worst moment in my life. I'm not being dismissive about the devastating nature of the crash and its aftermath, but it doesn't compare to the pain of personal loss.

My first wife Mavis was just 25 when she was diagnosed with cancer. It was 1961 and she'd discovered a tiny lump in her breast, a pea-sized cyst. I have to admit that around this time I had become completely obsessed with football. Now, however, my entire focus shifted to Mavis. I sold the gleaming Jaguar that had been my pride and joy. It was nothing but a status symbol. I was not normally ostentatious and, as far as I was concerned, it was taking me away from what had got me there in the first place. Material things were irrelevant, they merely emphasised the need to concentrate again on what really mattered. I was travelling to Old Trafford by bus and in order to take Mavis to the hospital for her biopsy appointment I had to borrow Benny Sternberg's car. I went back to pick her up a day later and as I pulled into the car park I spotted Mavis at the window waving down at me. I waved back and as I walked through the door the matron pulled me aside and said the surgeon, Mr Godfrey, needed to have a word. He said: 'I'm terribly sorry, your wife's tumour is malignant. We'll have to remove her breast.' I didn't know what to do, what to say, or how to face my wife. The medics told me to go and speak to her, but I just wanted to run away. I went back down the corridor, out the door, and headed quickly to the car. When I looked back Mavis was still standing, smiling at the window. Eventually the nurse persuaded me to return. I made my way to her room, but just couldn't find the words that needed to be said. It was Mavis who spoke: 'I'll be okay as long as you're here.'

Mavis had the mastectomy. She recovered wonderfully well and we went to Ireland for a holiday. On our return I took her for her final scheduled check-up. Instead of a clean bill of health, the medics said the cancer had spread. Each Tuesday after that I took her to Christies' Hospital for chemotherapy, an ordeal Mavis undertook with remarkable courage and fortitude. Over the following year my wife's condition deteriorated. She was admitted to hospital once again and communication was made difficult by the tubes which were inserted into her nose. One day she wrote down on a pad: 'Take me home'. The doctors were against the idea, but I did as she asked.

Mavis knew I was a fitness fanatic and she kept asking why I wasn't going to training. Fortunately I was sidelined with my shoulder, so I could give a genuine reason for staying at home to look after her. It was a tough time, too, for our young children. The two girls would often see me lifting mummy to the bathroom and would ask what we were doing. 'Mummy and daddy are dancing,' was all I could think to tell them. Eventually I informed Matt what was happening, although I still kept it from the general public. I even received letters from people in my own country accusing me of being too scared to fly to internationals, and of feigning injuries to miss matches. It hurt me deeply, but what could I do? I didn't want the truth to get out. I shut myself off from the rest of the world. She was mine. I alone would take care of her. Late at night I would go out to church and pray. And through it all I never once believed she was going to die.

Mavis passed away on 11 January 1962. I made the funeral arrangements, then took the kids by the hand and went to Altrincham Ice Rink. As they skated around, blissfully unaware, I sat and cried my eyes out. I'd always been a religious man. In fact, it was something which had helped me through Munich. But now, my faith was shattered. That morning, in my grief I told my mum: 'If that's Jesus Christ, you can keep him.' I know it hurt her deeply.

I was a physical and mental mess. I didn't care about anyone, or anything except my kids. I looked after the two girls with the help, and sometimes hindrance, of a succession of housekeepers. I hid my true feelings for the sake of the children. I'd lost my wife and I'd lost God. I couldn't even seek solace in football. In fact, had Mr Cregan not agreed to perform the shoulder operation that saved my career, I'm not sure what would have happened. The procedure was a gamble, but I had nothing else to lose.

I found myself on a downward spiral that threatened to get out of control. I lived like a tramp, walking the streets in a daze. I recall one occasion when I arrived home completely drenched, then climbed into bed with my clothes on. The following morning I got up, washed, shaved, changed, and went off to training as if nothing had happened. I was leading a double life. At one stage I asked the club could I buy the house I was in. They agreed, but only if I paid the market value. That was enough for me to change my mind and instead Jimmy Nicholson moved in and, more than ten years after arriving in Doncaster as a young professional footballer, I moved back into digs.

Mrs Scott's digs, which had previously been occupied by Pat Crerand, were situated near the club doctor Brian McHugh. Brian and his wife Teresa used to invite me and the kids over to spend some time with them and their three children. Eventually, though, I thought the best course of action was to take Linda and Karen over to Ireland and leave them, temporarily, in the care of my mother. Brian and I became great friends. I was due to attend the Manchester United versus Manchester City match which raised funds for the Duke of Edinburgh Field Awards and, with no-one to accompany me, Brian suggested I ask the girl who lived next door. Her name was Carolyn, and she was the only child of John and Sadie Maunders (the Maunders family were one of the north's leading building contractors who had built many of the houses on the Cheshire side of Manchester). I didn't know it then, but Carolyn would eventually become my wife.

It's hard to put my finger on one moment, or one thing, that brought me back from the brink. Mentally and physically, I can perhaps point to a row I had on the road from Sale to Manchester when trying to edge out of a side road onto the main drag. That morning I was feeling very low, in fact I was thinking: 'You're finished this time, Gregg'. Then a lorry driver began to hurl abuse at me. I jumped from the car, leaving it abandoned in the middle of the road, and started to run after the lorry that had come to a halt at the traffic lights. I tried to rip the door off its hinges, but the lights changed and it drove off. I returned to my car and carried on to Old Trafford. Many years later I told my mother and brother that this incident was the best thing that could have happened to me. It stirred me in a way totally disproportionate to the actual event. What it had done was to make me realise that I still had some fire left in my belly.

Dr Brian McHugh was a friend when I really needed one, and for that I'll always be grateful. There were others, too, who tried to reach me when I was down. After my shoulder operation, just as I was coming around, one of the nuns who cared for the patients in St Joseph's Hospital, Sister John, was on her hands and knees beside my bed cleaning the floor. She started talking to me, although not in an overtly evangelical way. I said: 'Sister, there's worse ways to die than on the cross.' Not the most sensible thing to say to a nun I have to admit, but every ounce of faith had drained away after my wife's death. Over the next few days a priest kept calling with me. He was a patient himself in St Joseph's, in fact he was terminally ill. Still he came to see me. I asked him if God was so all-powerful why did he have to prove it? He tried to explain his take on this particular question, saying that when a child sees the sparks from a fire he or she is naturally curious and reaches out. The father says not to do that. A few minutes later when the child puts his or her hand out again, the father smacks it. The child wonders why dad doesn't love him or her. It's an explanation that didn't convince me then, and still doesn't, but I respect his intentions. The nuns also brought me books, two of which stick in my mind – *The Man Who Got Even With God*, and *God Visits Death Row*. Maybe I didn't realise it then, but these people were reaching out to me, trying to help me the best they could. At no stage did they attempt converting me to Catholicism, they were just trying to restore my faith in God.

Months passed after my first date with Carolyn and I was pleasantly surprised when she came to visit me in hospital. I was back in St Joseph's again, this time recovering from a serious car crash. I always remember one of the nuns saying to me: 'Harry Gregg, that girl's far too young for you.' Carolyn was only 21. Not long after I got out I was walking, with the aid of a stick, from Brian McHugh's to my digs. Carolyn pulled up in her car and offered me a lift. I declined, but not long afterwards I asked her on a date. Our relationship slowly progressed and as we became more serious about each other certain issues raised their head. I was a widower with two children, and much older. Carolyn insisted her parents didn't mind, but I was not so sure. I asked her to arrange for me to speak to her father, but on three occasions he failed to keep our appointment. One evening I went into the Maunders bungalow and asked if I could have a few words. He turned in his chair and told me if I hadn't come to see him, he was going to find me. I reminded him that I'd made three attempts to do just that. The evening didn't end in confrontation, but it became clear Carolyn's parents had reservations about her seeing me. Eventually it came down to a choice and, against the better judgement of her parents, she chose to go with me.

We bought our first house together and one day after training I was decorating and noticed Carolyn was quieter than usual. I asked what the matter was and she replied: 'Will I always be second best?' She told me her mother had suggested she would be nothing more than a housekeeper if we married and I made Carolyn get her coat and go with me to her parents. As we approached a roundabout Carolyn said it hadn't been her mother. I stopped the car and told her she could keep the engagement ring. Finally, Carolyn admitted she was trying to protect her mum, and that Mrs Maunders did indeed have concerns about the marriage. When we arrived I did my best to clear the air, to put my side of things, and after our wedding in July, 1965, Carolyn's parents were nothing but supportive to me and the children.

I do consider myself to be a very fortunate man. I have a wonderful wife, a wonderful family, a wonderful life. It has been a nomadic existence, but such is the lot of the footballer, coach, and manager. Yet, even if the decisions I made were wrong, and on occasions they were, Carolyn was at my side. I was not wrong in her eyes. We've been together now for nearly 40 years and I'm the first to admit that living with me is far from easy. In fact, according to Carolyn I get more like Victor Meldrew every day.

VI

BETWEEN THE STICKS

I think it's fair to say my goalkeeping style was more Barthez than Bob Wilson. Unconventional, a little eccentric even, there were times when I was more gung-ho than Rambo. I dived where you weren't supposed to dive; strayed into territory off limits to most keepers; and commanded the 18-yard box like a gang member protecting his turf. If the ball was there to be claimed, heaven help anyone who got in my way. Even from the early days I believed I would be handicapping myself if I sheltered under the crossbar.

Agility, a necessity for any keeper, always came naturally to me. As a youngster I took part in gymnastic displays with Coleraine YMCA on a cliff top in County Antrim called Ramore Head. In the years to come I might not have scored too heavily on artistic impression, but that understanding of my physical limitations always stood me in good stead.

Of course, my zealous approach to the art of goalkeeping did have its drawbacks. Let's face it, if you throw yourself at the feet of forwards and plough through crowded goalmouths, you're going to get hurt. Injuries were the bane of my career, although I suppose I only have myself to blame. To be frank, I just didn't know any other way to play. Cup final or friendly, it was all or nothing.

Take the Kevin Doherty Testimonial match in my home town of Coleraine on 18 May 1954. Kevin, the brother of Peter (my boss at Doncaster), had been an accomplished player in his own right. He signed for Major Buckley's Wolverhampton Wanderers as a 14-year-old, played his first full match for the Midlanders on the day the Second World War broke out and gave sterling service to several clubs on the Emerald Isle. It was his eight years at Coleraine FC which prompted the testimonial, and with Peter pulling the strings on the mainland, a star-studded line-up was assembled. There was my Doncaster and international colleague Len Graham; Leon Leuty, the England centre-half; United's Jackie Blanchflower; Bertie Peacock from Glasgow Celtic; Everton's Davy Hickson; and George Eastham, who earned notoriety for helping to abolish the maximum wage through his landmark case against Newcastle United and the game's governing body. As for the forward line, well, it consisted of John Charles, Kit Lawlor, Peter Doherty and Raich 'Horatio' Carter. In a contemporary context, it was like having Giggs, Beckham, Keane and Michael Owen over for a kickabout.

The match was 25 minutes old when the ball broke between me and Jimmy Delaney. Jimmy was in the twilight of a career which included league and cup winners' medals with Manchester United (England), Celtic (Scotland), Cork City (Republic of Ireland) and Derry City (Northern Ireland). As usual I took no prisoners. Bang! We collided like rival stags. It was a sickening clash and after the dust had settled we were taken on stretchers to the dressing-room for treatment. I resumed in the second-half. Jimmy, on the other hand, left for hospital with a broken jaw and minus several teeth. The whereabouts of the wayward molars was explained to him when I visited the next night. He was only just coming around, and I was informed that his teeth had actually been embedded in my knee.

I'm not proud of this tale, or any other that involved someone getting injured. Then again, nor am I apologetic for the way I played the game. I was happy to live and die by the sword. It was a man's game after all.

When I joined United the current custodian was, of course, Ray Wood. As goalkeepers we were like chalk and cheese. Ray was calculating, a fine keeper in his own right, but an introvert to my extrovert. The defence at Old Trafford soon learned that the new boy wasn't going to stand on ceremony. Ten minutes into my debut against Leicester City I came for a high ball and collided with Duncan Edwards. Anyone else and they'd have been calling for a stretcher, but big Duncan just dusted himself down and said: 'Keep coming!' It didn't take the newspapers long to notice this reluctance to remain on my line. Not long after the Leicester match I found myself in a Manchester derby for the first time. As I looked up the pitch to my opposite number, Bert Trautmann, I was desperate to impress. Bert was one of my heroes and without doubt the greatest goalkeeper I've ever seen.

Red and blue halves of Manchester enjoyed equal bragging rights after a 2–2 draw, although I did suffer the indignity of being chipped for one of City's goals. Nevertheless, I wasn't too displeased with my display as I thumbed the pages of the *Football Pink* and *Football Green* on the train back home to Doncaster (where I was still living). Then a cartoon caught my eye. It was a caricature of me. I was tied to a totem pole with Matt Busby and the other United players dancing around me. The caption read: 'Have United bought a goalkeeper, or an attacking centre-half?' It played on my mind for the rest of the weekend and on Monday I went to the boss. I wanted to explain that these excursions were part of the Harry Gregg make-up. With a half smile he said that's why he'd signed me in the first place. It was just what I needed to hear.

Matt Busby and Peter Doherty were almost unique in their perception of the goalkeeper's role. Both realised that he was more than just a stopper, that he could be the eyes of the back four, the instigator of attacks. They gave me the licence to dictate and create. With the entire pitch spread out before him, the keeper was in a privileged position. I suppose I did for Matt what Peter Schmeichel would do for Alex Ferguson – act as an on-field director of operations. Matt and Peter also understood the need to command your area. I recall one of Peter Doherty's team talks prior to Doncaster's match with Leeds United. The formidable John Charles was the Yorkshire club's centre-forward and Peter told our centre-half Charlie Williams he'd no chance and not to bother taking him on. He proceeded to go through our entire defence one by one, telling each to hold their ground. Then he looked at me and said: 'Young man, you can beat him, come for everything.' Not only was it a massive vote of confidence in a young keeper, but also tactically astute.

In 2000 I went to a commemorative dinner with many of my ex-colleagues. During his speech, Noel Cantwell looked in my direction and said: 'Greggy, over there, was the finest goalkeeper. The opposition were terrified of Harry, but I'm not sure his own defenders weren't more afraid.' I doubt if anyone in the room had even the slightest inkling just what that meant to me. To be appreciated by Peter Doherty, or a peer like Noel is, in my book, the ultimate accolade.

Life between the sticks was tough but, boy, could it be rewarding. The thrill of making a crucial save, the roar from the fans, it was hopelessly addictive. There is no better feeling than listening to thousands of supporters chanting your name behind the goal. The Stretford End would even chant your name when you were out through injury. It's the same today, with Eric Cantona's name ringing around Old Trafford long after his departure for pastures new. In the '50s and '60s the United faithful were just that, faithful. Two hours before kick-off they'd be packed outside the Warwick Road end. Often when I would leave the ground an hour and a half after the final whistle they would still be outside in their droves looking for autographs.

I enjoyed the backing of the supporters. Others have been less fortunate. Take Jim Leighton. He became the butt of some serious stick. Different players respond to supporters' abuse in different ways. Take our full-backs, Shay Brennan and Tony Dunne. You could call Shay every name under the sun and he'd just turn and smile. Tony, on the other hand, tended to take criticism from fans or colleagues more personally. With one it required a good old-fashioned kick up the backside, the other a consoling arm. Incidentally, Shay's nickname, Bomber, originated from the one occasion when he didn't turn the other cheek. I was playing centre-forward in a training match at The Cliff. At one point the ball looked to have crossed the line and Shay and I exchanged a few words. Anybody else in the club and I wouldn't have turned my back. The next thing I was wondering what had happened as Shay landed one on me. He started running, and when it had registered with me just what he'd done, I took off in hot pursuit. By the time I'd caught up with Shay, 20 players had caught up with me. I fell to the ground under their weight, with Shay landing on top of me. Jack Crompton forced his elbow across my throat, but I bit a hole right through Shay's tracksuit. In the bath afterwards I sat on my own in one corner, whilst Shay soaked himself in the opposite corner, surrounded by his team-mates. The next day Matt called us into the referee's room. He reminded us about the family spirit at the club and asked what happened. Neither of us spoke. Anytime we met after that Shay would make a fist, and I would hold up my hand and say: 'Sorry, Bomber!'

Banter between fans and goalkeepers has always been part and parcel of the game. At Stamford Bridge, White Hart Lane, Anfield, Highbury and Upton Park you expected your fair share of verbals from the terrace wags. The great Frank Swift taught me a valuable lesson about how to win over even the most ardent away fans. I put it into practice in a game against Everton at Goodison Park. Instead of hurling a bit of abuse back, as I would normally have done, I tried to appeal to that famed Scouse humour. One guy in particular had been calling me all the names of the day. I decided to wind him up and, noticing that he was smoking, asked for a fag. His witty riposte was: 'F—- off, you Irish bastard!' Eventually, though, he gave in and passed me a match and cigarette. I struck it on the goal post, lit up and surreptitiously had a few drags. Within minutes the Evertonians were chanting my name. Many of my teammates were of the belief that this was not an isolated mid-match puff. Mark Jones and Jackie Blanchflower swore I'd actually burnt them when I came to collect a cross. Okay, that cig at Goodison wasn't a totally isolated incident, but the truth is that most of the time they were victims of a prank. I used to take three or four ammonia ampoules onto the pitch with me in my cap. They resembled half a cigarette. Sometimes, when my teammates weren't looking, I would take one out and put it in the palm of my hand. Then, if they looked over I would give them a glimpse of it. They thought I was smoking and the rumour mill was stoked up a notch.

The odd blast of nicotine was nothing, though. I once played for Doncaster Rovers against Bristol City in the FA Cup while as high as a kite. I had dived at the foot of the post and my rib cage hit the woodwork. Rovers trainer Jack Hodgson helped me from the pitch. When I reached the dressing-room the doctor prescribed an injection of morphine to ease the pain and act as a sedative. Everyone returned to watch the game and I lay there in a semi-conscious state. Then Peter Doherty arrived. Unaware that I was heavily under the influence, he asked if I was ready to go. I was in cloud cuckoo land and, assuming he meant ready to go to hospital, I said yes. I rose gingerly to my feet and floated down the tunnel after Peter.

The boss returned to his seat on the bench and, on automatic pilot, I wandered back to my goal. Our left-back, Ronnie Walker, had deputised for me and when he saw this zombie he returned to his original position with a daft grin on his face. When Jack Hodgson noticed me he was horrified. He raced around the perimeter of the pitch to try and persuade me to come off and go to hospital. I had no intention of coming off now, in fact, thanks to that jab, I'd never been happier. Jack was a nervous wreck as I chain-smoked for the rest of the match. A few drags was the only way I could keep myself from dozing off. During any breaks in play Jack doused my face with cold water and shoved an ammonia pad under my nose, proving that occasionally they did fulfil a role other than as mock cigs. There was nothing fake about my spaced-out condition against Bristol City that day, though, and heaven knows how I lasted to the end. I didn't get away with it altogether, however, for one hack reported the incident as: 'The Case Of The Drunken Goalkeeper'.

Coping with that taste of the *high* life against Bristol City was a doddle, though, compared with two matches against Liverpool over an Easter weekend. Like Doncaster, Liverpool were a Second Division outfit at the time. Everyone was tipping them as promotion certainties and our first meeting on that holiday weekend was at Belle-Vue. The trouble began when Alick Jeffrey gave us the lead with a contentious goal. Jeffrey, known to the fans as The Wonder Boy, was a precocious talent. Alick made the first team at 16, broke his leg in November the followng year playing for England Under-21s against France in Bristol, and still managed to finish leading scorer without kicking a ball again that season. The Liverpool players and their huge travelling support were not, however, quite so appreciative of young Alick's ability. Soon fans began encroaching on to the pitch and the small band of police officers looked hot under the collar as they tried to maintain some semblance of control. This already volatile situation was further compounded when our centre-half Charlie Williams went up for a ball and dropped to the ground like a stone. Charlie, a black man with a broad Yorkshire accent – not a particularly common combination in the '50s – would of course become famous after his playing days as a member of television's *The Comedians*. We all knew he had a wicked sense of humour, although to be fair, he tended to leave his antics behind in the dressing-room. I ran from my goal to tell him to pick himself up and get on with the game. As I got closer I realised he was out cold. It didn't take long to figure out why. Lying beside him on the ground was a British Rail salt cellar. We managed to bring Charlie round and I deposited the salt cellar in the back of my goal. Little did I know that this was only the beginning.

Later in the match the ball went out for a goal kick and as I went to retrieve it I noticed a policeman struggling to keep supporters behind the perimeter wall. The next thing he disappeared over the wall. As I placed the ball down to restart play I felt a sharp, stabbing pain in the back of my knee. I looked down and saw blood running from a gash in my leg. Next to my foot was a British Rail table knife. I called the referee's attention to the knife, but he said: 'Pretend you didn't see it.' I called back: 'But ref, it's my leg!' I threw the knife in the back of the net to keep the salt cellar company. The referee, perhaps understandably, didn't want to antagonise the baying mob further. It was also clear he was keen to put as much distance as possible between himself and the crowd. I can't say I was too happy with his decision and before the final whistle blew I had amassed quite a collection of cutlery from the British Rail buffet car.

You can imagine what the newspapers would have made of such an incident today. However, the police advised me against speaking about it, fearful, no doubt, of inflaming the atmosphere for the return match at Anfield on Easter Monday. I was happy enough for our 1–0 win to do the talking and we virtually ended Liverpool's promotion hopes when we beat them again at Anfield. It was quite a performance, especially when you consider that we were down to ten men for most of the match, Roy Brown going off with a broken wrist. Such had been the threat of further crowd trouble that Henry Rose from the *Daily Express* actually stood on The Kop that day. Fortunately Henry was able to report that the only items thrown at me were hard-boiled eggs. If only I'd held on to that British Rail cutlery I could have made a meal of it.

At the end of that particular season I passed through Liverpool on the way back home to Ireland. I bought an evening paper and smiled to myself when I read one reporter's assessment that Liverpool's promotion push had foundered on losing points to lowly teams like Doncaster. I thought, that'll teach them to mess with me and my mate Charlie.

As a black player in the football league Charlie came in for some terrible stick from fans, and the occasional opposition forward. Our Charlie, though, was more than capable of giving as good as he got. He was physically strong, with a personality to match, and he wasn't averse to giving his own teammates a right rollicking if he thought they weren't pulling their weight. I recall one occasion when I was on the receiving end of Charlie's caustic comments. I dislocated a finger against Nottingham Forest and let out an almighty scream. Charlie came charging over to see what all the fuss was about. He thought I'd suffered a broken neck or something and when I informed him about my finger he was singularly unimpressed. He ordered me back in goal. I didn't argue, I think I was so shocked at his dismissal of the injury as trivial. Fortunately Jack Hodgson had also heard my scream and he came tearing around the pitch to put my finger back in. Even Charlie approved, because it didn't require the referee to stop the game.

It's always said that goalkeepers are a breed apart. And sure enough, whenever we meet one of the subjects that somehow always crops up is gloves. In fact, one of the last conversations I ever had with Frank Swift was about just that. It was the day before the Munich crash and he told me about this company in Ashton-under-Lyne where he'd bought his gloves during his Manchester City days. Swifty said I should visit them when I returned. Sadly, Frank lost his life in Germany. I made that trip to that shop in Ashton-under-Lyne – it was the least I could do.

Like most keepers I had my little quirks. If it was raining some would wear patterned gloves. I, on the other hand, preferred to turn them inside out so that the knots made the surface of the gloves rougher. On a dry day, instead of wearing gloves I would chew gum or a piece of orange and then spit in my hands to make them tacky. Anything was worth a go if it helped to make that ball stick. I'll never forget the trend for big gloves in the '70s. I think it was the West German keeper Sepp Maier who was the most high-profile 'big gloves' exponent during the World Cup in '74. Great in theory, but I don't think I'd ever seen as many shots palmed away in my life. It's a tactic still employed by most goalkeepers, even today, but not one of which I approve. A keeper palming a ball down to pick it up would have been in serious trouble in my day. Denis Law would have been in his element. He'd have nipped in and added another 100 goals to his season's tally.

I have to admit it's hard to beat having a chat with the lads who played with and against you during the '50s and '60s. I think we all appreciate that our game bears little resemblance to the modern manifestation. Even United's rivalries have changed. Today, it would probably be Liverpool, Arsenal, Leeds United and the men from Maine Road. By contrast, the likes of Leeds United had only been promoted back to the top flight towards the tail end of my career. It was 1964 when they re-joined the First Division and Jack Charlton was the Yorkshiremen's centre-half. It was Jack who instigated the tactic of standing in front of the opposing goalkeeper at corners, waving his arms in the air and generally making a right bloody nuisance of himself. It was intimidating and, in many instances, highly effective. Even today goalkeepers find themselves drawn to that physical presence like a magnet. Personally, I liked to deal with this particular situation without the assistance of my defence. I would place myself three or four yards beyond the back post, a move designed to confuse Jack. Then, when the ball was in the air, I would move forward like an express train. As he jumped up, you just buried man, ball, the lot. Taking each other's players out would become the modus operandi for the two Uniteds over the next couple of decades as the Manchester versus Leeds rivalry replaced the ding-dong affairs we had traditionally served up with our Lancastrian neighbours, Bolton.

I always enjoyed those tussles with the Wanderers. Unlike Leeds United there was never any taunting about Munich from the Burnden Park terraces. On the field, though, the rivalry was red hot. And believe me,

Bolton were a tough and talented lot. Roy Hartle, Tommy Banks, big John Higgins, Derek Hennan, Duncan Edwards' cousin 'little' Denis Stevens, and of course my old mate Nat Lofthouse. A few years ago, when United and Bolton were drawn in the FA Cup, it was decided to have a reunion of the '58 Cup final teams. Tommy Banks, a wonderful character, had been one of the Bolton full-backs. He was their team's enforcer and was known for shouting at his full-back partner Roy Hartle: 'Brother Hartle, if tha's havin' any trouble with friend Giles, send him over to brother Banks.' After the match Tommy and I met up in the boardroom. It didn't take long before Tommy, his broad Lancastrian brogue booming across the room, took over proceedings. The entire boardroom was in stitches with his antics. Then who should walk in but the actor Ian McShane, who's dad Harry had played for United in the early '50s. Ian, who is a lovely fellah, was introduced to everyone. Unfortunately, Tommy discovered who his father was and, not standing on ceremony, he said: 'Aye, lad, was thee dad Harry McShane the winger?' Poor Ian didn't know where to look, or what to say, so he just nodded. Tommy continued: 'When he heard the sound of my studs coming down the corridor he ran back up the tunnel.' Diplomacy was not Tommy's strong suit. Tommy's encore that day was to perform press ups on the boardroom carpet. No mean feat when you've had two hip replacements.

Tommy Banks was not the only tough character around. Being able to withstand the knocks that were regularly dished out was essential if you were to survive. Playing with a dislocated finger, or with cracked ribs, was one thing, but I also suffered injuries which were a genuine threat to my career. For a goalkeeper there's nothing worse than shoulder trouble. And I should know.

In a match with Tottenham Hotspur during their Double winning season (1960–61) I dived to save a shot from John White. It took a deflection and adjusting mid-air I landed with my hand on the ball, my full body weight coming to bear and violently jarring my shoulder. The pain was incredible and I initially thought it was dislocated. The trainer came on, told me it was okay and I attempted to play on. Minutes later a ball was pulled across the six-yard line and I dived. In football vernacular, it was a real 'hospital ball'. Unfortunately Bobby Smith caught me right on the same point of the shoulder I'd hurt moments before. My shoulder was now more prominent than nature intended and I had no feeling down one side of my body. I was taken to the medical room on a blanket and Ted Dalton, who was dressed in a dinner suit as he had an evening engagement, asked for someone to lie across my legs. Johnny Aston Snr lay across my left arm as Ted removed his shoe and tried to force my shoulder blade back into place. After a few minutes he stopped and announced that it wasn't going to budge. I pleaded with him to try again. He raised my arm, moved his foot back, and with a loud crack the bone finally realigned. As this was still the era before substitutes I had the shoulder strapped and returned to play the rest of the match at up front. It was at this time that I had my first meeting with Mr Cregan, a surgeon who would eventually save my career.

I was advised to keep the shoulder immobilised for seven weeks. Matt was in hospital for a back operation and Jimmy Murphy was in charge of training. I was trying to stave off the boredom by taking part with my arm strapped to my side. With two weeks of my rehabilitation still to complete, Jimmy and Ted Dalton asked me to speak to them in the medical room. Jimmy said he needed me to play. So, despite being far from fit, I took my place in goal against Nottingham Forest and then Manchester City. The newspapers heralded: 'Gregg the great is back,' but I knew it wasn't the real me. My complaints about the pain fell on deaf ears. It's just scar tissue and your imagination I was told. A few weeks later I paid the penalty for my hasty return during five-a-sides. I was playing outfield, as usual, and as I turned, my shoulder dislocated. Ted spent an agonising and ultimately futile 45 minutes trying to put it back. Finally they managed to track down Mr Cregan and I was packed off in a taxi, Wilf McGuinness wrapping me in a bear hug for the duration of the journey in an effort to restrict the movement and pain. Mr Cregan gave me an injection, put my shoulder back in and told me not to move my arm for seven weeks. 'Some scar tissue,' I said to Mr Cregan. He answered: 'It's a good thing it happened.'

On another occasion against Liverpool I broke my collarbone in the first-half. Jack Crompton, United's trainer at the time, came on, threw his arm around me and asked if I was okay. I don't think my reply was particularly polite, but suffice to say I drew his attention to the bone which was attempting to protrude through my jersey. I left the pitch, had it reset, then tied the arm of my jersey to a coat peg and wriggled back in. Ted Dalton and the club's orthopaedic surgeon Mr Alan Glass tried to stop me, but I returned to the match as a makeshift centre-forward. David Herd went into goal, whilst I tried my best to make a nuisance of myself against big Ron Yeats. I don't think my efforts were fully appreciated, though, for Denis Law said after the match that I'd bloody well got in everybody's way.

Eventually, my right shoulder packed in, big time! The injury was so severe I was forced to take a gamble in order to stay in the game. The club once more sought the help of Mr Cregan. He initially talked about an operation to have my shoulder bolted. Unfortunately, even if successful, it would permanently restrict my arm's movement to below shoulder height. He asked what else I could do with my life. What could I say? Football *was* my life. My wife had died and I felt there was nothing more to lose. It was then he mentioned a procedure that had been used on pilots who had suffered multiple dislocations during the war. Called the 'Putty/Platt', it was a complicated and unpredictable operation. It was, in his opinion, too risky. I refused to take no for an answer.

Mr Cregan successfully performed the 'Putty/Platt' and many years later I came across one of the nurses. She said he'd actually blunted the scissors in the operating theatre whilst trying to cut the piano wire which held my dodgy shoulder together. I had the operation in April 1962, and the following month I went home to Ireland to recuperate. I was shocked when I removed the bandages which had bound my arm from waist to neck. My pectoral muscles had completely wasted away. Over the next few weeks I spent as much time as I could standing on the banks of the River Bann. With a bandage tied to my wrist, the other end wedged between my teeth, I swung the arm to cast. It's a tactic I'd used before, and it worked.

My stubbornness, and Mr Cregan's skill, saved my career. And the price for some *extra time*? Well, it's the long, unsightly scar which snakes down my shoulder and stares at me every morning from the bathroom mirror. It looks like a shark bite and my children used to really love it when I told them the yarn about my scrap with Jaws.

As any sidelined player will tell you, it's a time when you rely heavily on your teammates. The other lads at United were great and I still enjoyed a game of five-a-side. Playing away with my one good arm wasn't the most sensible move, but it meant so much to me to know I could still be involved. If only the club had been as supportive as my teammates. Their idea of helping me get through one of the most difficult times I ever had as a player was to cut my wages. As a first-team player out injured you were entitled by contract to be paid your appearance money, and your crowd money, until such times as you were fit to return to action. Crowd money was a deal we had for a couple of seasons. It amounted to a payment of £2 per thousand for gates at Old Trafford between 32,000 and 42,000; and £1 per thousand for attendances between 42,000 and 62,000. The rest of the lads were on two-year contracts and I was on a one-year, so I went to see Matt Busby and raised the issue. The boss said: 'We'll take care of you, son.' I replied: 'What about now, boss?' Manchester United knew the prognosis was that I would be sidelined for 18 months and it really hurt when my new contract stated that I wasn't entitled to appearance or crowd money. This raw deal made me all the more determined to get back. My training took on a frightening intensity. I pushed weights when they told me not to. I pushed my body to the limits when they said I should be resting. And through it all I had also endured my fair share of mickey-taking from my teammates. On one occasion I shouted back that I'd be fit again when I got my appearance money. It was said in jest, in response to a jibe made in jest. It did not get reported that way to the boss. I was training away and was surprised to find that Matt was being very off-hand with me. In fact, he even turned his back on me. Eventually, I'd had enough. I met the boss and Jack Crompton in the corridor and I asked Matt: 'Why the needle?' Jack eventually realised this was going to be a private conversation and got offside. Matt said: 'Of all the men I've met, you're the one I'd put my life on. Did you say you'd play again when you got your appearance money?' I replied: 'Yes, I did, but it was said in jest.'

I was hurt that Matt would think I would seriously make such a remark and added: 'If one of the staff told you, I'll hold my hands up. If it was one of my colleagues I'll find him.' Matt told me to do nothing of the sort, but I was soon making enquiries. Jack Crompton said if anyone else had asked him, he would have ignored the question. As it was me, he'd answer. But Jack didn't know the identity. I spoke to Johnny Astor Senior and Bill Foulkes – neither could shed any light. Finally, I questioned another of my teammates. He told me he couldn't answer until he'd spoken to Jack Crompton. That was all I needed to hear and I told him not to bother. To have tales told behind your back by a colleague is hard to take, but I'm content in the knowledge that the man in question is aware I know. In the end I returned to action nine months ahead of schedule. My comeback game was in a seldom-mentioned friendly between Manchester United and Benfica.

Manchester United versus me and my stubborn streak was something of a theme, especially when it came to injuries. I accept responsibility for most of the knocks I've received, but there's one occasion which springs to mind when the needless wear and tear inflicted on my body was down to others. It started with a horrific car crash on the Crossford Bridge in Sale. I was at a function with Brian McHugh and a few of his mates from back home in Ireland decided to spike my drinks with poteen. I was teetotal at the time. I'd never have known what happened had it not been for a subsequent conversation with a girl who had been at the party. She rang me at the hospital to say she was worried about me. I asked why. She told me she had watched as the lads tampered with my glass (which had contained ginger beer and lime). Obviously the worse for wear I clipped a light pilon on the way home, sending my car careering out of control. It slewed across the road, knocked some huge rocks into the Mersey and ploughed into a car showroom's forecourt. Clipping the roof of two stationary cars, I was somehow somersaulted clear. As if in slow motion I looked down as the car broke up below me. I finally landed in the road. I should mention that my backside cushioned the fall, not a technique I would recommend. Sensing someone running towards me, and thinking back to Munich and Jim Thain's warning that the plane was going to blow,

I called out to turn off the engine. Some teenagers who'd been at Altrincham Ice Rink came over and laid their coats across me. I heard one of them say: 'Christ! It's Harry Gregg!' I saw a taxi approaching and shouted for someone to stop it. I crawled in and told him to take me to 61, Briarlands Avenue. When we arrived I realised my trousers had been ripped off in the crash and I didn't have any money. The taxi driver told me not to worry. 'After what you've been through, you deserve a free ride.' Now, I'm sure my actions appear like those of a complete madman, but believe me, I'd two very good reasons for not wanting to go to hospital. One was my kids, who were being looked after by a housekeeper. The other was Matt Busby. That afternoon I'd sat on the sidelines as a late Paddy Crerand goal salvaged a draw for us in the FA Cup against Sunderland. I'd been out with my collar-bone since the Liverpool game and Matt turned and said: 'No fitness test for you. You're playing Tuesday night.' How was I going to tell the boss I was crocked again?

I struggled into the house and tried successfully to make it upstairs. I looked in the mirror – it wasn't a pretty sight. Before long the doorbell rang. It was the police. After a brief discussion they persuaded this bloodied and sorry soul to go for treatment, not a bad idea considering I had a depressed fracture beside my left eye, a suspected broken leg, knee damage and a broken big toe. I phoned Brian McHugh and it just shows the grip Matt Busby had over all of us, because he too was worried about the reaction at Old Trafford. So much so that he asked me not to tell Matt he'd been at the party. There was no way I was taking the rap for this on my lonesome, so I signed myself out and went home. I lay in bed throughout the next day. Noel Cantwell came to see me and he told the lads back at United that I was lying there swathed in bandages like the Invisible Man. Eventually Mr Glass, United's orthopaedic surgeon, called and he immediately insisted I was admitted to St Joseph's Hospital. Forget about the pain, I was terrified what Matt would say if we lost to Sunderland. Fortunately Denis Law managed to secure another draw for us, although I was still keen to avoid explaining my current predicament to Matt. It was Wednesday morning, I was halfway out of bed in an effort to grab a quick look in the mirror, when who should walk in but the boss.

His first words to me were: 'In the name of God, how many lives do you think you have?' I said: 'Boss, I wasn't drunk.' Matt was also adamant there had been a woman in the car with me. There hadn't, but somehow that's the story which emanated from the crash scene. I mean, they even dragged the river looking for his non-existent woman. I told him it wasn't true and he said he'd talk about the crash more when I got out.

One leg bore the brunt of the injuries I sustained in the crash and to be honest I was struggling in training. I was trying my best to cover up my discomfort when Matt began heading in my direction. Some of the lads said: 'He's going to ask you to play.' They were right and I ended up making my comeback against Wolves. After the match Maurice Setters said to me: 'You're like a hen hopping across a midden.' Next up were Liverpool, our nearest rivals for the league title. It was at this time that the players decided to have a press blackout. Now, you can imagine how popular that was with United gunning for glory on three fronts. We were second to Liverpool in the league, in the semi-final of the FA Cup against West Ham United, and in the semi-final of the European Cup-Winners' Cup with Sporting Lisbon. The press turned up en masse at Old Trafford for a photocall and our club captain Dennis Viollet delivered the news of our media ban. There was a right commotion until Matt Busby appeared. He never raised his voice, but needless to say seconds later the snappers had their picture. We lost 1–0 to Liverpool. I knew my leg wasn't right.

Finally, Matt sent me to hospital where Mr Glass removed my cartilage. I was normally a quick healer, yet ten weeks later and there had been little or no improvement. I attempted to train, but when my leg gave way during a session of Sergeant jumps I decided to see the boss again. I tried to convince Matt that there was something wrong with my leg. You didn't give Matt Busby ultimatums, or demand things, but I said I would appreciate a second opinion. He told me that wouldn't be easy. Ted Dalton added that Mr Glass might be offended if we second-guessed him. My career was on the line, but heaven forbid we would annoy the club surgeon who, incidentally, was a lovely man and a dear friend.

Two weeks passed. Then I received the message that Alan Glass was going away on holiday. United were due to play Fulham and I was told to travel with the team to London so that I could attend Sir Oswald Clark, the Queen's surgeon who, as it turns out, was a native of Belfast. By this stage Matt and I weren't on speaking terms. That was often his way when players were out injured, it wasn't just me. He felt that if you were injured it was your fault and he treated you accordingly. I'm also convinced he felt my problems were psychosomatic. We arrived at the President Hotel and, as per my instructions, I waited at the reception desk. Matt arrived, carrying a large brown envelope containing my medical records. We got a taxi to Harley Street, with not a single word exchanged between us the entire journey. The sombre mood didn't last for long, though, and it was me who had the last laugh.

We hadn't been sitting that long in the waiting area when a bell rang and the receptionist, clearly not a football fan, said to Matt: 'You can go in now, Mr Dalton.' I smiled to myself as a visibly annoyed Mr Busby disappeared into the surgeon's office. I was petrified at the prospect of meeting Sir Oswald and with every passing second I became more and more convinced Matt was inside portraying me as some big daft Irishman with an imaginary injury. Eventually, I was called. I could tell by the look on Matt's face that he was expecting the surgeon to confirm it was all in my head. Sir Oswald asked who had performed the cartilage operation. I told him Mr Glass. He said: 'Yes, yes, posterior horn.' Well, I don't know who was more gobsmacked, me or Matt, when he added: 'Unfortunately you also have a broken fibula.'

It's a miracle I can get up in the mornings when you consider the battering my body's taken over the years. Life between the sticks certainly took its toll, not only in terms of injuries, but also matches and medals missed. But I don't have any regrets about playing the way I did. After all, it opened the door to not only a career with Manchester United, but also 25 treasured appearances for my country and the title 'best goalkeeper' at the World Cup in 1958.

VII

SWEDE DREAMS

There was a feeling of enormous pride, tinged with considerable relief, when I heard the news in 1954 that I'd been chosen to play against Wales in a World Cup qualifier at the Racecourse Ground, Wrexham. Northern Ireland selectors Sammy Walker and Jim Rock had been to watch me in action for Doncaster Rovers reserves and I'd very nearly scuppered my chances of a first cap by rashly giving away a penalty. Now, having represented my country at every other level, I was on the verge of completing the set. Of course, it wouldn't be me if I didn't manage to fit in a spot of drama along the way.

The plan was that myself and Len Graham (Doncaster Rovers and Northern Ireland full-back) would travel down on the Sunday to meet up with the rest of the squad at our headquarters in Rhyl. Unfortunately, I played for the Reserves against Gainsborough Trinity on Saturday and picked up an injury. In saving a penalty I'd deflected the ball into the path of a Trinity player, leaving me with no alternative but to dive at his feet. His stray boot inadvertently caught me in the back, and the pain increased during the night. Instead of heading to Wales on Sunday, I was forced to report to Doncaster's ground for some much-needed treatment. Jack Martin sent for Peter Doherty and it's fair to say my club boss, and also my country's manager, was not best pleased. He sent Len on ahead to Rhyl as planned and ordered me to accompany him to Port Vale on Monday. Peter was scheduled to play in an exhibition match for the Old Internationals and he arranged that I could have treatment at the same time. A big Australian called Ken Fish looked after me whilst Peter paraded his considerable skills alongside the likes of Joe Mercer and Bill Shankly, heroes I'd gawped at, all wide-eyed and innocent, in the dressing-room earlier that day. After the match, and with my back still throbbing, we left for Rhyl to link up with what I hoped would be my new teammates. Peter marched me into the dressing-room and, looking around, I suddenly spied a familiar face. The last time I'd seen this particular player was as a 17-year-old playing in the Enniskillen Cup (one of the many highly competitive summer cup competitions in Ireland where many professional players took part without permission from their clubs). We faced a Dundalk Select and I nicked the ball ahead of their centre-forward. Just as I cleared downfield their outside-left came past and kicked me on the back of the legs. I saw red and chased him to the halfway line where the situation was eventually calmed down. I hadn't seen him since. It was Peter McParland.

I was still in some discomfort when match day arrived. So, before taking the field I was whisked off to the bathroom. With me holding on to the water taps for support they gave me a pain-killing injection in my back. Whatever was in that syringe, it did the trick. I did well against a Welsh forward line led by John Charles. Having played against him for Doncaster and been boosted by one of Peter's inspirational pep talks, I was confident enough to come for everything. My former sparring partner Peter McParland did his reputation some good too, for he scored both our goals in a 2–1 win, Northern Ireland's first in Wales since 1923.

I played again for my country against the Combined Services, but there was a gap of nearly three years before I won my next full cap. By this stage I'd established myself as the number one at Doncaster and was receiving rave reviews for my displays in a side struggling to stay in the Second Division. The selectors had clearly noted my consistency and pencilled in my name for the Home International Championship clash with England at Wembley.

If our record in Wales was less than impressive, then our chances of success in London were, at best, remote. In fact, we had to go back 30 years to find our last success over England, a 2–0 win at Windsor Park. For a young man like myself the whole experience of playing England at

Wembley was intoxicating. I'd watched England international matches on Pathe News, now here I was the day before our game walking around an empty Wembley with my teammates. I can't speak for the rest of the players, but I was beginning to feel the enormity of the approaching match. Nerves, though, were easily dispelled when you had a man like Gerry Morgan around. Gerry, our trainer, was an amazing character. Hardly the epitome of health and fitness, he was bald, had only two front teeth, and quite clearly liked his food. And Gerry didn't so much kiss the blarney stone as swallow the bloody thing whole. As we strolled around the selectors chatted about how great it was for Northern Ireland to be here at this historic stadium to play England. Gerry piped up: 'Great, my arse, sure greyhounds have been running here for a 100 years.'

The night before the match we went to the pictures and Gerry, known to all the players as *uncle*, was up to his antics again. During the film he would shout things like: 'Look out, he's behind you!' The usherette would come down, shine her torch and ask for him to keep quiet. Danny Blanchflower also added his admonishment, but with his brother Jackie egging *uncle* on there was more to come. His *pièce de rèsistance* succeeded in bringing the house down. There was a commotion and the next thing we knew the lights had come on and then the film stopped. There was Gerry, hanging off the back of the seat, screaming to the usherette that he'd seen a rat. The lads were in stitches, laughing. I don't know whether Gerry deliberately did these things to take our minds off the game, but that's the effect it had. And I have to add that he also managed to pull off one of the great acts of deception. A player and trainer with predominantly protestant club Linfield, a man who appeared to be a true blue, when Gerry died he was actually buried in a republican cemetery.

In truth, the Northern Ireland set-up at that time was brimming with wonderful characters. Jack Gaw, one of the selectors and chairman of Irish League club Bangor, had an opening line he used at all functions that the team attended. Jack, with his tweed suits and distinctive handle-bar moustache, would stand up and say: 'My name is Jack Gaw. I make Kest [a laxative] for a living and our slogan is "Kest for zest". But my slogan is: "Billy Graham saves souls, but Jack Gaw saves arseholes."' Now, that's what I call an ice-breaker.

As for the game itself, well, we seemed to be on a hiding to nothing. England, on paper at least, looked to be leagues apart. Johnny Haynes, who for me is one of the greatest players to ever pull on an England shirt, was joined up front by Tommy Taylor – Duncan Edwards and Roger Byrne bringing the United contingent to three. Billy Wright was captain, and there was also Derek Kevan, Alan A'court, Don Howe and Ronnie Clayton. It looked odds on that the English would continue their hoodoo over Northern Ireland.

As I stood in the tunnel waiting to be greeted by that famous Wembley roar, I was reminded of just how far I'd come by England captain Billy Wright. He made a point of coming over and shaking my hand. Clearly remembering me from that match at Windsor Park when I conceded nine goals to Billy and his English League colleagues, he said: 'You've come a long way, son.'

It turned out to be quite a match. We beat England 3–2, the last ten minutes taking what seemed like an eternity to pass. I must have asked the referee a thousand times how long there was to go as England surged forward in search of an equaliser. The Northern Ireland fans invaded the pitch on the final whistle and we were chaired off Wembley's famous turf. On a personal note my display attracted newspaper headlines. It was a thrill to pick up the papers and read: 'Magnificent Gregg sees Ireland through to victory', or 'Great Gregg inspired great win'. More importantly, though, this win provided the catalyst for our World Cup campaign, Northern Ireland's first. Peter Doherty and the Northern Ireland selectors had gambled on bringing in youth, with the likes of Billy McAdams, Billy Bingham, Jimmy McIlroy, Peter McParland, Jackie Blanchflower and myself all coming in from '54 onwards. They would reap the rewards as we started on the long road to Sweden.

When the World Cup qualifying draw pitched Northern Ireland into the same group as Portugal and Italy it seemed that an appearance at the finals in Sweden was nothing more than a foolish pipe dream. It didn't take any great expertise to predict that the *azzurri* would clinch top spot, after all, they were already twice winners of the Jules Rimet trophy. Our track record could not have been more contrasting. In fact, we didn't have one. When we boarded the plane to Lisbon we were effectively stepping into the unknown.

Straight from the kick-off under the floodlights of the Jose Alvarez Stadium the Portuguese made no attempt to disguise their rough-house tactics. With the French referee prepared to take a lenient approach, it was clear this was going to be a baptism of fire. The situation reached almost comical proportions when their right-back grabbed Peter McParland by the collar and ripped the shirt from his back. Not long afterwards the same player almost killed Peter with an attempted knee-high tackle he did well to avoid. Billy Bingham gave us the lead, Northern Ireland's first World Cup goal, with a cracking volley after only five minutes. However, Vasquez equalised when I misjudged a cross in the lights and palmed the ball straight to his feet. At the next corner I was doing my usual directing. I was saying what players needed to be picked up, adding that the lights were bad. Tommy Casey turned to me and said: 'The only one who can't see is you!' I lost it and started running after him to the halfway line, pulling my jersey off as I went. I don't know quite what the Portuguese thought of it all as I offered to let Tommy try to do better. In the end we had to settle for a hard-earned draw. It had been a physical encounter, yet amazingly, worse was to come later in the campaign.

Next up was Italy in Rome's vast, majestic Olympic Stadium. With huge statues peering down from the lip of the stadium bowl, it was enough to intimidate even the most seasoned professionals. Like Wembley, few gave us a chance, especially as Jackie Blanchflower and Peter McParland were missing due to the impending FA Cup final between Manchester United and Aston Villa. To compensate for their loss, Peter Doherty pulled a master stroke. He picked diminutive Wilbur Cush, the most underrated player in the history of Irish football, at centre-half. Wilbur didn't give their centre-forward, Charlton Athletic's Eddie Firmani, a kick of the ball all game.

The form I'd shown against England was replicated in Rome. Cervato beat me with the game's solitary goal, but only after he'd moved the ball a few feet and taken the free kick before anyone could object. The Italian fans gave me an amazing reception coming off the pitch and their generosity continued when I went to a sports shop in the city. The shop owner handed me a pair of new boots and said: 'For you, Mr Gregg, take them.' My performance also attracted the interest of Italian club side Genoa. John Charles had just transferred to Juventus and he came to the match and suggested afterwards that I might soon be following in his footsteps. Not according to Peter Doherty, though. On the flight home he informed me that I'd be going nowhere. He said when I moved it would be to the right club, as he saw it.

The return match with Portugal at Windsor Park in May saw no repeat of the antics in Lisbon. Tommy Casey, Billy Simpson and Jimmy McIlroy scored to complete a relatively comfortable 3–0 win. Jimmy's penalty was a real talking point because Danny Blanchflower was the actual spot-kick taker, but instead he ingeniously tapped it to one side and Jimmy did the rest. Everything was now set up for the showdown with Italy on 4 December 1957. At stake was a place in the World Cup finals.

Windsor Park was full to bursting. More than 58,000 fans crammed in, each champing at the bit for the first whistle. Who could blame them? This was uncharted territory for fans and team alike. The only thing that was missing as kick-off approached was the referee. Hungarian Istvan Zsolt (stage manager of the Budapest Opera House) had missed his cue and was fogbound in London. When it became clear he wasn't going to arrive, feverish discussions took place between officials of both teams. The Italians, perhaps understandably, refused to accept the official use of a local referee, Lurgan man Tommy Mitchell, and it was decided to reduce the match to *friendly* status. Without the prior knowledge of the IFA officials, the news was announced over the tannoy. The crowd, who'd paid to see the biggest game in our history, were not going to be easily placated. The chorus of boos which greeted our entrance left none of us in any doubt as to the prevailing mood on the terraces. If passions were running high off the pitch, on it the Italians did little to assuage the growing tension. They took great exception to a shoulder charge on their keeper

Bugatti by Billy McAdams and the game quickly degenerated. Billed as a friendly, it became anything but. Cervato scythed down Billy Bingham, then Juan Schiaffino, the former Uruguayan international, enraged the crowd further with an horrendous tackle on Wilbur Cush. All over the pitch there were verbals, sly punches and kicks. It was a war. At one stage two fans ran on to the pitch to confront the Italian captain Ferrario – he dropped both of them. Peter McParland then appeared to clip their goalkeeper and Italy's right-half Chiapella went berserk. He drove his feet into Billy McAdam's back and all hell broke loose. Italy pulled back our two-goal lead, but even that failed to take the heat out of the situation. Chiapella was eventually sent off, but poor Tommy Mitchell had long since lost control of this match. The final shrill blast of his whistle should have ended what would become known as the battle of Windsor. Unfortunately for the Italians, the nightmare was only just beginning.

Supporters cascaded on to the pitch as the Italians headed for the sanctuary of the dressing-room. The baying mob had the scent of blood in their nostrils and starting attacking the Italian players. As Eddie Firmani headed down the tunnel some fans called him over to the fence. They held his hands and pushed the fence against his face, causing a bad gash. I was one of the last to leave the pitch and, I have to admit, I wasn't particularly worried. The way I saw it, I was wearing a Northern Ireland jersey. I was one of them. It never entered my head that they'd try to hurt me. I've read various accounts of what happened next, with different Italian players mentioned. I know for a fact that the player involved was Bene from AC Milan. I heard him crying and went over. I put my arm around his shoulder, thinking that would be enough to protect him. Then an arm came over my shoulder and whacked him with a stone. Down he went, and in the spur of the moment I began laying into anything that moved. I kicked and punched until the police arrived on the scene. Bene was eventually returned to his teammates, who by this stage were standing on the benches and hanging on to the window ledge of their dressing-room. They thought we'd done the damage to their player and I decided it best not to wait around to explain.

When the dust had settled the Italians maintained they would never play at Windsor Park again. Questions were even raised in their parliament. Eventually, though, FIFA insisted there would be no change of venue and on 15 January 1958, Northern Ireland and Italy stood toe-to-toe again for the right to go to Sweden. Once again fog played a part. Only on this occasion I missed the match.

I'd played the evening before for Manchester United in the 3–2 European Cup quarter-final win over Red Star Belgrade at Old Trafford, receiving special dispensation from Matt Busby to travel straight away to Belfast. I made it as far as Manchester's Ringway Airport, but all flights were grounded. At one stage it was suggested I might be able to get on board a plane delivering the pools coupons, but even that was prevented from taking off. I ended up sitting in the terminal with a photographer, Bill Gregory, watching the match on television. It was one of the most frustrating moments of my life, eased only slightly by our 2–1 win. The Cinderella nation had earned the right to go to the ball. But our greatest hour was yet to come.

The decision to play in the 1958 World Cup was not one I took lightly. The fact that some matches were scheduled for a Sunday presented me with a very real dilemma. I'd been brought up to believe in the age-old tradition of strict Sunday observance. Apart from attending church, just about everything else on the Sabbath was a real no-no. The football authorities didn't exactly help when it came to making a decision. After all, in March the previous year the Irish Football Association had themselves actually agreed to an article banning Sunday soccer. At one stage it even looked as though Northern Ireland might not compete in Sweden at all. With vociferous anti-Sunday-soccer campaigners like John Cassells stirring the pot, I tortured myself over what was the right thing to do. Finally, during one of United's training sojourns to Blackpool, I decided to seek some divine guidance. I looked through the local phonebook, found the number of a church in the town, and phoned the vicar. I explained who I was and what was troubling me, and asked if I could come and see him. We talked and the one thing which struck a chord with me was when he asked whether I thought it was sinful for a surgeon to save the life of my child on a Sunday. I left with conscience at least partially salved.

Although the Munich crash had happened only a few months earlier, I never ruled out flying to the World Cup. However, the IFA pre-empted any agonising over that particular decision by making my travel arrangements for me. I went to Sweden by sea and land, accompanied by one of our selectors, Joe Beckett (who, because of his religious beliefs, turned right around and went back home). Most of the journey was spent sitting on my luggage and I arrived safe and sound at our picturesque headquarters in the seaside resort of Tylosand. It was here that Peter Doherty hatched his plan of attack, a strategy which succeeded beyond all expectation. There was little evidence to suggest we could make any sort of impact, particularly as our already slender squad (we'd lost Jackie Blanchflower because of his Munich injuries) was reduced to 16 when Glasgow Rangers' Billy Simpson pulled a muscle which ruled him out for the entire tournament. With Leicester City's Willie Cunningham switched from full-back to centre-half and Derek Dougan replacing the hapless Billy Simpson, we made the short trip to Halmstad, venue for our opening match against one of the tournament's dark horses, Czechoslovakia. Little Wilbur Cush latched on to a quickly taken short corner between Billy Bingham and Jimmy McIlroy to head the only goal of the game. It was the boost to morale we'd all hoped for.

Halmstad's compact riverside stadium was once more the venue for our second match against Argentina. The South Americans could have been forgiven for thinking they were running out at Windsor Park. The local populace had adopted us as their own and number-one fan was a 13-year-old from Tylosand, Bengt Johansson. Son of a wealthy local businessman, he followed me everywhere. I remember his tears on the day we left, and me lifting the youngster high above my head. A wonderful little lad, he was later invited over to Belfast. It was at the time that my first wife was critically ill and I couldn't attend. I always regret having to make the lame excuse that I was injured, but I couldn't tell anyone the real reason.

If the Czech match was followed by understandable euphoria, the 3–1 defeat by Argentina brought us back down to earth with a hefty thud. There was little chance of the downbeat mood remaining for long, though. In addition to the wise-cracking Gerry Morgan, we had Mickey

McColgan for company. Mickey and Newry man Leslie Nicholl rode a moped all the way to Sweden, then pitched the tent which had been strapped to Mickey's back on the lawn of the hotel. They lived there for a few days until some of the lads arranged to get them a room. It became a home from home for us all, Mickey holding court as he made cups of tea on a Primus stove.

With Mickey and a small band of Northern Ireland supporters (including David McGrotty and Frankie Harte from my hometown, and former Coleraine player Stanley Mahood) supplemented by Halmstad's growing gang of honorary Irishmen, we travelled to Malmo for the all-important meeting with West Germany. Facing us was a side led by 38-year-old Fritz Walter, who four years earlier had received the Jules Rimet trophy from the man himself. Highly organised and supremely confident, the Germans boasted a powerful blend of youth and experience. As the klaxon horns of 10,000 fervent followers of the Fatherland filled the air, the moment of truth had arrived. We took the match to our illustrious opponents, Peter McParland giving us the lead after 17 minutes. Sadly, in instigating that particular attack Tommy Casey picked up a knock and had to leave the field. Minutes later Helmut Rath equalised for the Germans. Back we came, Peter grabbing his second of the match. As West Germany pushed for an equaliser it was time to stand up and be counted. Fortunately, this was to be one of those days for me when I hit top form. Despite the fact that I'd damaged ankle ligaments in the first few minutes (I persuaded Gerry Morgan not to take off my boot, so he strapped ankle, boot and all) it was one of those occasions when you felt unbeatable. I remember one moment when the ball was floated across, just outside the box, and I took my cap off in mid-flight to head the ball just before Uwe Seeler. The local rag ran the headline: 'The Miracle Man of Malmo', and we looked like holding on for a famous victory until Seeler beat me with a stunning strike. A draw was enough to book our place in phase two, though both myself and Tommy Casey were now added to the list of players sidelined with injury.

Norman Uprichard replaced me in goal for our second match with the Czechs. The match was only one minute old when Bertie Peacock was forced to leave the field with knee ligament damage. Wilbur Cush, who was limping himself, still managed to set up Peter McParland for his fourth goal of the campaign, and he added a second to seal the tie. Amazingly, the smallest nation of the 53 who started on the road to qualification had made it to the World Cup quarter-final.

Back at Tylosand the hotel was like a casualty department, with Dr Scarlett and Gerry Morgan working overtime. Free-scoring France lay in wait and with just 48 hours until the match there was scarcely a player left in the squad who could claim to be 100 per cent fit. Nevertheless, we were up for it. In fact, we firmly believed it was our destiny to meet Pelé and the Brazilians in the final. If our injury crisis placed us at a distinct disadvantage, so too did the World Cup schedule. For the West Germany match we'd travelled 100 miles up less than perfect roads; now for the quarter-final we had to up sticks and move to Norrkoping. The French, by contrast, had four days' rest and no change of HQ.

Norman Uprichard had broken a bone in his hand against Czechoslovakia, ruling him out. The hospital said I'd be out for eight weeks, but with six hours a day spent bathing my ankle in the healing properties of sea water my recovery was well ahead of schedule. I threw away the stick I'd been using to walk since the German game and played. We held the highly fancied French for almost the entire first-half, but the team was now running on empty. Raymond Kopa began to utilise the space that was now opening up and two goals from Just Fontaine (who finished with a tournament record tally of 13) and one from Piantoni ended the Northern Ireland fairytale.

What we achieved under Peter Doherty should not be underestimated. It was a seminal moment for small nations. We proved that a country with only a million and a half people could cut it with the big boys. Funny, despite setting such a precedent and achieving so much with so little, many people in my own country seem to think Northern Ireland's World Cup history begins in 1982. I've nothing but respect for what Billy Bingham and his squad achieved in Spain, but Peter Doherty and the class of '58 deserve to be remembered.

Personally, the World Cup exceeded even the wildest dreams. I was voted Best Goalkeeper in the tournament, ahead of the likes of Lev Yashin, the legendary Russian stopper. And I remain deeply honoured also to have been chosen for the World XI, polling more votes than a young lad called Pelé. Only a couple of years ago an IFA official was in France for a youth tournament. Just Fontaine was there and he asked about Harry Gregg and Bertie Peacock. To hear something like that, to know you made your mark, is very special indeed. I also ran across Fritz Walter and Uwe Seeler at the 1998 Champions League final in Munich, men I respected and who, I was delighted to learn, respected me.

The notoriety I received after the Munich air crash, allied to that match with Seeler and Co. in Sweden, has forged a unique bond. I still, to this day, receive letters from fans in Germany (and from around the world). It's correspondence I read with great pride and then add to the wad of envelopes already stored in a cupboard at home. One German man sent me a letter about a friend whose trademark was a yellow roll-neck sweater. He wore it everywhere because that's what I wore in goal. Then there are the Essen Kickers, a group of over-50s who formed their own club. During the World Cup in the USA they met up with a man from Sion Mills and asked about Harry Gregg. The Essen Kickers then came to Ireland in order to meet me. And one of the most touching tributes I've ever received came from the vice-chairman of Bayern Munich, Hans Schiefele. He was working as a newspaper reporter in Munich on the night of the crash. Herr Schiefele said in an interview with the *Daily Mail* in 1998: 'The thing that people may not realise is that, in a way, Manchester United were our team, too. To us in Munich they were a role model because they were so far ahead of Germany. Above all, it was Harry Gregg, the goalkeeper we loved.' The esteem in which I'm held in Germany has always meant a lot to me.

The 1958 World Cup was a watershed for Northern Ireland and for my career. And the journey home also proved to be of immense significance. With everything that had happened in Sweden I was on a total high. Although arrangements had been put in place for me to travel home by land and sea, I made the decision to fly. I went to Peter Doherty and said: 'Boss, if you can get me on a plane, I'd like to fly home.' He asked me if I was sure, then went to see IFA Secretary, Billy Drennan. They took me off the train, straight to the airport and on to a plane. Fortunately, I was not booked on the same flight as the rest of the squad. Their aircraft took off from Stockholm, but due to a technical problem, it was forced to circle the Swedish capital for two hours, jettisoning all remaining fuel before making an emergency landing.

To be brutally frank, I'd no idea how I would react. Slowly, we taxied down the runway. By the time we were airborne the arm rests on my seat were saturated in sweat. I was content to suffer in silence until the captain came over the intercom: 'We're delighted to have on board Munich survivor and World Cup star, Harry Gregg.' Then the steward arrived with a drink for me. Anonymity was now out of the window and the woman next to me began chatting. She was a bookie's wife from Southampton who had been in Stockholm on holiday with her friends. Well, when she got started, that was it. For the entire duration of the flight she hardly took time to breathe. My old friend Sammy Walker was also on that flight, along with Jack Doherty and Jack Gaw. A few years ago, not long before Sammy passed away, we got talking about old times. He asked me if I remembered the woman from Southampton who bent my ear during that homeward journey from Sweden. I said: 'I think I do. I thought she was never going to shut up.'

VIII

A BAD BET

I always considered it a privilege to be paid for playing football. But with that privileged position comes a certain responsibility. Call me an idealist, but I firmly believe that each and every player, coach, and manager is duty bound to do their best. We owe it to the game, and to those not blessed with the skill and opportunity that takes you to the top. Sport, though, like most walks of life, is open to corruption. And the greater the prize, the greater the temptation. Canadian sprinter Ben Johnson was rightly pilloried for cheating his way to the gold medal in the Olympic 100 metres. But what is the greater crime, taking a pill to enhance performance, or taking a bribe to under perform? For me, the biggest cheats are those who sell out their sport, who let greed overcome integrity. We all know that football has been blighted by game sellers and bung takers. George Graham is one of the most high profile examples of the latter, but by no means the only one. A man richly rewarded for his efforts, the ex-Arsenal boss allowed himself to be lured by the filthy lucre. And yet, Graham is back in the game. He has even been welcomed back into the fold by the media, past crimes ignored. To see him employed as an analyst, or co-commentator, hurts me. For those who have dragged football's name into the gutter should never again be allowed within 100 metres of any football ground. And football falling foul of the rule breakers is not a modern phenomenon. During my own playing career I witnessed events every bit as despicable as those in the modern era.

British football was stirred and shaken on the morning of Sunday, 12 April 1963, when three Sheffield Wednesday players – Peter Swan, Tony

Kay and David Layne – were cited for match-fixing in the *People* newspaper. The article revealed that Swan, England's centre-half, Kay, who was also capped after moving to Everton, and 'Bronco' Layne, as he was known, had conspired to throw a match against Ipswich Town in December the previous year. Wednesday lost 2–0 and Messrs Swan, Kay and Layne were eventually convicted, banned from football for life and sent to prison.

This was no isolated incident. Jimmy Gauld, the former Everton forward, admitted two other matches had been simultaneously fixed (Lincoln against Brentford in the Third Division and York against Oldham in the Fourth). More players were implicated and rumours circulated that this was only the tip of the iceberg. The truth is that games had been thrown long before the Sheffield Wednesday three were exposed.

Season 1962–63 was not a particularly memorable one at Old Trafford. The club had embarked on the long road back after Munich and was finding the going tough. Relegation was a very real possibility and performances on the pitch brought stinging criticism in the press. Steve Richards from the *Daily Herald* penned an article in which he slated: 'A bunch of party wallers who were letting the great Matt Busby down.' I went to see the boss and told him I was going to call a meeting of the senior pros. He listened to what I had to say about the cliques that had developed amongst the players and told me he would set-up a meeting if I got the players to talk. In all we had three such meetings. After each the situation temporarily improved, before once again degenerating. And it was during this time of internal turmoil that Manchester United came under investigation by journalists regarding rigged matches, although nothing ever appeared in print.

A goalkeeper is better placed than anyone to influence the result of a match and I suppose it was inevitable that the men involved in match-fixing at Old Trafford would approach me. The first time that I became aware that something was going on was when young Dubliner Joe Carolan came to me for advice. I was totally caught by surprise when Joe, who I must stress was not involved, asked for a quiet chat. We went into the boot room and he said: 'Have they been to see you yet?' I asked what about and he told me they'd offered him the chance to earn some extra readies on the fixed games and he didn't know what to do. I replied: 'They won't come to see me,' and advised Joe to 'Go deaf, son.' I was wrong, though. They did approach me. This not so subtle recruitment drive took place in the treatment room at Old Trafford. I had been waiting for treatment from Ted Dalton when two established players brought up the subject of match fixing. Every time Ted popped out they chatted as if I wasn't in the room, casually mentioning there was a few bob to be made. I said: 'Here, that's the second time I've heard that. If I hear it again I'll be straight upstairs and you won't have to bloody ask who told.' The two men in question said I was mad, not the first time that had been levelled at me, and that they'd only been kidding.

Nothing more happened until an incident at the Norbreck Hydro in Blackpool which threatened to blow the whole thing wide open. We trained in Blackpool once every month and I was standing in the hotel's foyer when two *Daily Mail* reporters walked in. They introduced themselves, which was unusual because I knew all the sports hacks. It transpired they were news reporters and they said they knew I'd stopped United throwing games. I walked them along glass alley (as the windowed area which ran along the front of the hotel was known) and down beside the swimming pool. You're always wary of the press, so I answered their allegations with: 'Thanks for the compliment, but I'm not that big a man.' They explained further what they'd uncovered and ended up enlightening me. If I'd doubted that games had been thrown, I was becoming more and more convinced. You don't throw teammates to the press pack, though, so I repeated that they had the wrong man and left. I then gathered as many of the team together as I could. I warned them that two reporters were sniffing about and that they were just waiting for someone to bite. I said I didn't want anything to do with it.

Our visit to Blackpool coincided with a match at Bloomfield Road between the Irish League and their English counterparts. Jackie Milburn, then player/manager with Linfield, was captain of the Irish League; and Bert Trautmann was set to become the first foreign player to represent the English League. Danny Blanchflower was dispatched to cover the match by the *Sunday Express* and he was standing at the reception desk next to the *Daily Mail* newsmen. To the left of the foyer, at the cloakroom, was Wilf McGuinness. The *Mail* reporters began talking about how terrible the selling of games was for football; their voices were quite deliberately raised. Danny was clearly annoyed and said: 'I sincerely hope you're not suggesting Tottenham Hotspur.' The reporters replied: 'No, but I'm afraid we can't say the same for your brother's club.' On hearing this, Wilf, who was on crutches, went across and confronted them. He threatened to tell the boss, which, according to the press pair, was fine by them because they'd been trying to talk to Matt for two days.

Back at Old Trafford I had a quiet word with Jack Crompton. It was clear from his reaction, though, that he hadn't a clue what I was on about. Eventually I went to see Matt Busby. I knocked on Matt's door, something we were never supposed to do. The normal procedure was to ring first and ask if we could speak to him. Matt was sitting behind his big desk and I pre-empted the conversation by telling him there was no way I was giving any names. He asked me what I was on about and I said I didn't mind having lumps kicked out of me, but I wasn't sure who was playing for us or against us. He ranted and raved, saying over and over: 'I bloody knew.' And this was from a man not noted for his histrionics or foul language. Obviously, I'd merely confirmed what Matt already suspected. The proof that he knew something had been going on came in a letter from the editor of the *Daily Mail* apologising for the behaviour in Blackpool of his two reporters. Matt read it out to us and it's the only time, aside from Munich, I actually felt sorry for him. What a blow to your pride, to your respect for what had been built at Old Trafford. And yet, there was nothing he could do. I've no doubt that if Matt did not believe the match-fixing rumours were true he would have instantly sued the *Mail.* It was a case of no smoke without fire.

Incontrovertible proof of the match-fixing came in 1964. If I'd been in any doubt that my teammates had thrown games, I wasn't after a chat with one of the men involved. He'd been upset about a completely different matter and, as I dropped him off in the car, our conversation got around to the subject of match-fixing. He admitted he'd done it and named the others involved. I left Manchester United in 1966 and I know that after my departure games were thrown.

Thirty years later and a match-fixing storm would again threaten to destroy the very soul of the game. In March of that year the police arrested Bruce Grobbelaar, John Fashanu and Hans Segers. I knew Bruce well, our paths first crossing when I was manager at Crewe Alexandra. I received a letter from the Vancouver Whitecaps about a player who wanted the chance to prove himself in England. They wanted me to take him on trial. I agreed, but by the time he arrived I had departed Gresty Road for a job as coach at my old stomping ground, Old Trafford.

Dai Davies, who had played under me at Swansea City before moving to Crewe, called me one day to tell me about this young goalkeeper. He was convinced I would like him. I saw Bruce play at Port Vale and, eventually, we met when I was in Crewe for my eldest daughter's wedding. I'd gone into town to cash a cheque and decided to roll by the ground. Standing outside was Bruce Grobbelaar and I went up and introduced myself. It was arranged with Tony Waddington that Bruce came to United for ten days and after his short stint was over I went to Dave Sexton and recommended that we sign him. Dave didn't take my advice and a few months later, after Bruce had returned to Canada, Bob Paisley flew out and recruited him for Liverpool.

Bruce and I spoke on and off during his time at Anfield. He would ring for advice and I helped him in any way I could. I was staggered when, in 1994, the *Sun* devoted six pages to Bruce and match-fixing allegations. Knowing Bruce and the pride he had in his goalkeeping, I find it difficult to accept he threw games. I do admit, though, that the secretly recorded video of him and his former friend and business partner, Chris Vincent, looked damning.

I was inadvertently caught up in another potentially dangerous and technically prohibited scam during the '60s – the selling on of Cup final tickets. It was something that was rife in the game at the time and it certainly didn't have the stigma or seriousness attached to it that it would today. In the era of the maximum wage cap, it was looked upon as a necessary top-up. Even at the height of our powers professional football

CHILD'S PLAY: I was proud as punch to win my first cap for the Irish Schoolboys as a 14 year old. I could never have imagined that over the next seven years I would be capped at every level for my country (Schools, Youth, Amateur, Inter-League) culminating in my first full cap in 1954.

SCHOOLBOY'S DREAM: The Irish Schoolboys team which beat their Welsh counterparts 2–1 at Coleraine on 17 May 1947. I'm standing (back row fifth from right) and two to my right is a young lad called Jackie Blanchflower. It was to prove the start of an enduring friendship between two 14 year olds who would eventually fulfil every schoolboy's dream by playing for Manchester United.

FIRST TO THE PUNCH: In action for Doncaster Rovers, who I transferred to from Coleraine in 1952 for the princely sum of £1,200. I'm beating Leyton Orient's Tommy Johnson to the ball and on the extreme right is my teammate Charlie Williams, later to find fame as a member of the hit television series *The Comedians*.

THE MODEL PROFESSIONAL: Eat your heart out David Beckham. Television ads and photo shoots may be *en vogue* with the modern footballer, but we dabbled a bit ourselves back in the '50s.

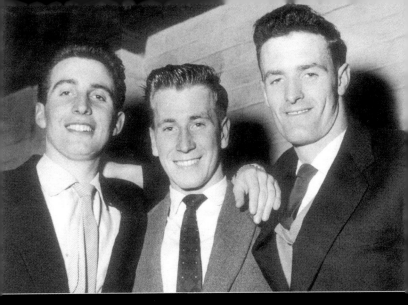

YOUNG AT HEART: There was a tremendous spirit amongst the Busby Babes. It seemed like nothing could stand in our way. (From left) David Pegg, Bobby Charlton and Liam Whelan.

PRACTICE MAKES PERFECT: Getting my fingers burnt in training by a Duncan Edwards blockbuster. Duncan was a brilliant player – and who knows how good he could have become?

A MOMENT IN THE SUN: They were a group of young men with everything to play for, everything to live for. (From left: Johnny Berry, Liam Whelan, Dennis Viollet, Mark Jones, Tommy Taylor, David Pegg and Wilf McGuinness.) Liam, Mark, Tommy and David lost their lives at Munich.

NEXT STOP MUNICH: This photograph was taken on 2 February, 1958, as we boarded the plane at Ringway bound for Munich. (From left: Walter Crickmer (Secretary), Duncan Edwards, Frank Swift (journalist), Albert Scanlon, Ray Wood, Dennis Viollet, Archie Ledbrook (journalist), Geoff Bent, Liam Whelan, Mark Jones, me and Kenny Morgans.) Of the eleven men pictured here, only four set foot on English soil again.

THE FINAL LINE-UP: Anxious moments before kick-off against Red Star Belgrade. This is the last photograph of the Busby Babes together before the crash. (From left: Duncan Edwards, Eddie Coleman, Mark Jones, Kenny Morgans, Bobby Charlton, Dennis Viollet, Tommy Taylor, Bill Foulkes, me, Albert Scanlon, Roger Byrne.)

THE MORNING AFTER: A bewildered Bill Foulkes and myself survey the scene of devastation that greeted us the next morning on that slush-covered runway in Munich.

MY SAVING GRACE: Just 13 days after the crash Bill Foulkes leads us out at Old Trafford to play Sheffield Wednesday in the FA Cup. Bill and myself were the only survivors from the team which took the field in Belgrade. Playing again saved my sanity.

ALL THAT REMAINED: This was what was left at Old Trafford after the crash – backroom staff and players. (Front row from left: Joe Armstrong (Chief Scout), Bill Inglis (Assistant Trainer), Jimmy Murphy (Acting Manager), Jack Crompton (Trainer/Coach). Second row from left: Johnny Giles, Colin Webster, Tom Spratt, Ernie Taylor, Shay Brennan, Alex Dawson, John Mooney, Mark Pearson, Reg Hunter. Third row from left: Fred Goodwin, Bob English, Reg Holland, Ronnie Cope, Harold Bratt, Bobby Harrop. Fourth row from left: Barry Smith, Ian Greaves, Bill Foulkes, Peter Jones. Back row from left: Gordon Clayton, David Gaskell, me.)

Opposite Page (Bottom): HOLLOW VICTORY: The vacant expression on my face, and that of Bill Foulkes sat to my left, says it all. We had beaten Sheffield Wednesday, but there was no sense of elation, just an all-pervading numbness. (From left: Ronnie Cope, myself and Bill Foulkes, Jack Crompton, Ian Greaves, Freddie Goodwin, Shay Brennan.)

RE-UNITED: My emotion-charged reunion with Verena and Vesna Lukic, the Yugoslav mother and daughter I'd pulled from the wreckage at Munich. (From left: Ian St John, Martin Tyler, Verena Lukic, Vesna Lukic.)

NEW YORK, NEW YORK: The Manchester United party en route to New York in May **1960** on board the *Queen Mary*. (Back row from left: Alan Gibson (Director), Jack Crompton (Coach/Trainer), Bill Foulkes, Alex Dawson, Joe Carolan, me, Frank Haydock, Albert Scanlon, Matt Busby. Front row from left: Harold Hardman (Chairman), Tommy Heron, Nobby Lawton, Johnny Giles, Mark Pearson, Shay Brennan, Albert Quixall, Ronnie Cope.) It was on this trip that I had the opportunity to meet world heavyweight boxing legend Jack 'The Manassa Mauler' Dempsey.

was far from lucrative. I'm not complaining, but the truth is that from
Matt down we were paid a pittance compared to the modern game. For
example, in 1966 when we reached the European Cup semi-final against
Partizan Belgrade there was considerable interest among the players as to
what we might be paid for the two legs. I was rooming with Denis Law
and just as I left Matt passed me in the doorway. When I returned to the
room a few minutes later Denis had a face on him like a wet weekend. He
said. 'Do you know how much we're getting for the two games? Sixty!
Sixty quid!'

When it came to Cup final tickets the players followed the same system
every year. A committee was formed, usually comprising the strongest
members of the first-team pool at the time. They would then set a price
for the tickets and no one was permitted to sell under that figure. It was a
defence mechanism inspired by the roasting Manchester City players
received at the hands of one shady dealer back in 1956. He'd promised the
City lads cars in exchange for their tickets. But when the final was over the
players found out he'd bought the cars on hire purchase. Consequently the
United lads didn't want to be ripped off. When Bill Foulkes, Roger Byrne
and a few of the other players were caught dealing tickets a year later, it
was decided that a closely controlled committee was the way to go.

At United some of the senior lads formed a committee to look after the
sale of tickets. We each received two complimentary tickets for the stand,
and two for the paddock, plus there was an option on another ten. This
was a new situation to me because at Doncaster you were lucky to get just
two.

In 1958 both Bobby Charlton and myself had been away on
international duty when the Cup final tickets were handed out. Everyone
else had handed their spare tickets over to the middlemen by the time we
arrived to collect our allocation. We were told to go into town and do our
own dirty work. Bobby, who was wearing a long tweed overcoat, took me
to a bookmaker at the back of London Road Station. There we met this
huge lump of a man with glasses – and his minders. On the ticket
envelope was written the number of tickets multiplied by the price. The
bookie looked at the envelope and then announced that there had been a

call over since we were away and the bottom had dropped out of the market. He offered us a lower price and straight away I asked for my tickets back. He refused – I asked again. Then he advised me to speak to Bill Foulkes. He dialled the number and handed me the phone. Bill confirmed that when we were away the committee had changed the price. As I was listening I noticed Bobby backing away. Before long he was right up against the electric fire on the other side of the room, his lovely coat now in danger of catching alight. The penny hadn't dropped with me and I thanked Bill and put the phone down. I accepted the bookie's offer, took the money and was escorted across the road to a Vauxhall dealership. Bobby agreed to buy a red Vauxhall Victor; I plumped for a blue one. After the deal was sorted out, I asked Bobby why he'd been backing across the room. It was only then I realised just how confrontational I'd been in that room. And believe me, these were not the sort of blokes to get shirty with. When I was haranguing these heavy characters to get the tickets back, Bobby had decided that caution was most definitely the better part of valour.

One of the bookie's muscle that day was a bloke known to us. A United fanatic with a reputation for his nefarious activities, he eventually ended up in Dartmoor Prison. This was a guy who, like Norman Stanley Fletcher from *Porridge*, regarded jail as an occupational hazard. Some years later he did attempt to make it up to Bobby. He loved United players, and none more so than Bobby, so he sent Mr Charlton a shield carved whilst under lock and key. Poor Bobby didn't know what the hell to do with it. He daren't throw it away in case this guy turned up on his doorstep someday. It wouldn't surprise me if it's hanging in Old Trafford today.

IX

THE LIKELY LADS

The Munich crash left Manchester United with no option but to rebuild. Initially it thrust into the limelight players not previously associated with the first team at Manchester, their promotion from reserves and youth team accelerated out of necessity. Others were drafted in from outside Old Trafford as Matt Busby and Jimmy Murphy laid the foundations of another United dynasty. These Likely Lads had one thing in common, they carried a huge burden of expectation.

Nothing can quite prepare you for the scale of things at Manchester United, where crowds of 20,000 and 30,000 turned up to watch the reserves, where tradition and heritage could cling around the neck like a millstone. Some rise to the challenge; others crumble and fade away.

In the Theatre of Dreams few stars shone brighter than Denis Law. Signed from Italian club Torino in August 1962, for a British record fee of £115,000, Denis became the darling of the Old Trafford terraces. I first saw him during my Doncaster days. He played for Huddersfield Town alongside the likes of Dave Hickson and a more unlikely looking footballer you never saw. He was terrifyingly thin, like a leek, but it didn't take a genius to see that Denis Law was something quite special.

Off the field Denis was a completely different person to the one who displayed such fire and bravado during his day job. Even now, when required to do after-dinner speaking, or appear in company, he'll still come across as cheeky, chirpy and full of confidence. But it's an act, something he turns on, rather than it being his natural way. Denis is a quiet lad at heart, more of a thinker than his extrovert alter ego would suggest. He has always been his own man, even at United, where Matt Busby was the archetypal authoritarian. If Denis made up his mind about something, nothing, and I mean nothing in God's earth, could shift him. Take injuries. The rest of us might have been easy to talk into playing if we were carrying a knock. Not Denis. Matt's presence in the dressing-room was enough to sway most at least to test their injuries in training. However, this tactic failed miserably with our Denis. Matt would ask: 'Would you not give it a go, son?' Caesar, as I always called Denis, would just stand with his back to the boss and say nothing. In his own good time he would then change into his kit, stroll down the tunnel, do about half a lap, and walk straight down the tunnel again past Matt. Then he would change and leave . . . all this without a word being exchanged.

On the field Denis Law had few peers. He was a truly great player, and I don't use the word 'great' lightly. He had complete and total command of his reflexes. No matter how a ball came to him, particularly in the opposition goalmouth, he would get in a strike. It didn't matter which part of his body, he'd connect. His awareness was uncanny; it was as if he had some sixth sense which enabled him to read the minds of his teammates and opposition defenders. He was the master of the one-two, which he used to devastating effect, and there was no one braver.

Bill Shankly once said of the flame-haired Peter Doherty, whom he played with for the Combined Services: 'The ginger Tom! Whenever he played in front of you, you didn't get a kick of the ball. He stopped them, started them and scored them.' When Denis first arrived at Old Trafford he was that sort of player. All action, all over the pitch. He was, in my eyes, the complete inside-forward. Matt Busby, though, had other ideas, and I remember the day he transformed Denis into a purely attacking weapon. We'd been going through a rough patch, our performances not matching Matt's expectation. Then during one team talk, he announced: 'From now on Denis Law does not come back over the halfway line.' I thought to myself, that's a waste, this guy's got so much to offer all over the pitch. In the end Matt was right. Denis went on to become an even more prolific goalscorer: his 236 goals in 393 games for United is all the evidence you need.

He had been troubled with a cartilage injury originally picked up at Huddersfield Town and watched the match with Benfica from his hospital bed. Denis felt the medical staff and others were suggesting that much of the trouble existed in his mind, even though he'd complained constantly about pain in his knee. Denis gave the boss short shrift when he went to visit. I called on Caesar myself in St Joseph's and he told me that when Matt had asked how the leg was he'd said: 'Do you want to see the scar?' then pointed to the side of his head. Whether that remark was true or not, I don't know. But it would have been typical of Denis.

Denis eventually left Old Trafford, swapping the red of United for the sky blue of City. Few will forget that back-heeled goal that sent his former club down, or what was probably the most muted reaction from a goalscorer in the history of football. Before his departure for Maine Road I actually attempted to sign him for Shrewsbury Town, a saga which hinged on another player, Alf Wood. I'd moved Alf from centre-half to centre-forward, where he scored a club record 42 goals in one season. I'd also gambled, at least in the eyes of the board, on bringing in the unproven Jim Holton to replace Alf at the back. Alf's exploits in front of goal were attracting considerable attention from other clubs, among them Bill Shankly and Liverpool. Bill phoned me and asked what we wanted for him. I told him £75,000. The following day I had a telegram from Bill McGarry at Wolves, who was in New York, asking me to do nothing until he returned. Behind the scenes Ted Fenton of Millwall was also chasing Alf and the Shrewsbury board, fearing that their player might be a one-season wonder, decided to sell. I can tell you, Bill Shankly was not a happy man when he found out. He offered to pay the £75,000 price I'd first stated, more than the board had settled for from Millwall, but the Shrewsbury board refused to go back on their word and the deal stood. The transfer did provide me with some money to spend. So I decided I'd make some enquiries about Denis. I asked the board how much I had to play with. They told me £20,000. I then enquired as to whether they objected to the money going to a player, as opposed to a club. They gave me carte blanche to spend as I saw fit.

Frank O'Farrell was in charge at Old Trafford and Denis found himself out of the team. I was assured by old friends of Denis that he was not a happy chappy. A circular came around stating that United had players in all positions available for transfer. I rang Frank up and we chatted. He spoke about players in the 'A' team, 'B' team and reserves, but I told him there was nothing there that I wanted. I said: 'It's for you to tell me who's available', but I couldn't force him into an answer. So I told Frank I'd take Charlton, Law and Best. He replied: 'You're very funny.' I added: 'Sure Denis is not in the team,' and he asked whether I thought Denis would go. I decided to play my cards close to my chest and didn't enlighten him any further. Nothing came of our discussion, but on the Sunday night I left the house, went down to Gay Meadow, locked the door to my office and phoned Denis. Diana, his wife, answered and told me to call back because Caesar was in the bath. It was a difficult few minutes because this was a call I didn't particularly want to make. I was not Harry Gregg, friend and former team-mate; I was Harry Gregg, manager of Shrewsbury Town. I was going to ask one of the greatest players ever to don the red shirt to drop out of the top flight and move to the modest surroundings of Gay Meadow. I eventually spoke to Denis and after a bit of banter I told him I'd £20,000 and asked him if he fancied a move. Denis replied: 'Give me the number of the pub you're in, for that must be strong ale?' Joking aside, Denis did not altogether rule out the idea. He was worried, though, about missing out on the testimonial he was due at Old Trafford. So the following day I went to see Matt Busby, who was a director at the time. I admitted talking to Denis and mentioned the testimonial. Matt assured me that if I looked after the player, he'd sort out the testimonial. Unfortunately, that was as close as I got to signing Denis. Within a few days Frank O'Farrell was gone. Tommy Docherty took over and Denis was back in the team – for the time being at least.

I consider Denis Law a good friend. I respect him as a player and as a person. I'm not suggesting there weren't other lads around whom I trusted, but Denis is the sort of fellah whom you could really depend on. In fact, there are not many people I would say this about, but I'd bet my life on him.

Denis was dubbed 'The King' by his loyal subjects on the Stretford

End, but not everyone enjoyed such an exalted position. Some couldn't cut it at Old Trafford, others, like Johnny Giles, chose to seek pastures new to receive the true recognition their talent deserved. In that, Gilesy was something of a rarity, a player who proved his worth in Manchester, but became a star only after he left to join Don Revie's Leeds United. Yet it shouldn't be forgotten that he was also a brilliant player for United. I've heard all this talk that it was money which lured Johnny away from Old Trafford, but my reading of the situation is that he moved because he felt, as the youngest player in the team, he was still being treated as the apprentice. He also preferred to play as an inside-forward, whereas Matt played him on the wing. Johnny actually went to Matt and asked to be placed on the transfer list, which few people did at Manchester United. Within the space of less than 24 hours Don Revie was on the phone. I'd been friendly with Johnny and he came to see me. He asked if I knew anybody at Leeds. I rang Bobby Collins from the kiosk phone in the corridor at Old Trafford outside the dressing-rooms and made a few enquiries. A day later Johnny Giles had departed for Yorkshire. Ironically, he would take over at inside-forward from Bobby Collins.

I've heard people say it was at Elland Road where Johnny developed that abrasive edge to his game. That's not the way I see it. Even at United he could handle himself. You see, Johnny was on the receiving end of a few bad tackles early in his career. He then clearly decided what was good for the goose was good for the gander. Johnny would leave his boot in all right.

Aside from his ability as a player, the other thing I will always remember about Gilesy is that he was, without doubt, the biggest practical joker during my time at United. He would take the piss incessantly. At training he might place himself just within earshot, then mutter: 'Dopey bastard, I think he's a bit weak on his left-hand side.' If questioned he'd deny everything, then a few minutes later he'd be winding you up again. To be fair to Johnny, though, he was also a tough little so-and-so. I once saw him hit Bill Foulkes. Bill, who was twice his size, warned Gilesy he'd hit back if he ever did it again. So what did Johnny do? He smacked Bill again. Bill repeated his threat . . . and John repeated the punishment. Matt Busby just stood there watching, his mouth wide open in amazement.

Gilesy just couldn't help himself. Even when he could see he had wound someone up to breaking point, he couldn't resist pushing it that little bit further. On one occasion it led to myself and Wilf McGuinness having a set-to. Every Friday morning after training there would be a 'head tennis' competition in the gym, a two-a-side game of one-touch control. Wilf and Bill Foulkes had won it for 19 weeks on the trot and they were really rubbing it in with the other lads. Johnny came to me and asked if I would partner him against Wilf and Bill. Johnny's close control was immaculate and before long we were well in the lead. Our opponents were none too happy with the way things were going, especially as Johnny never shut up. He kept asking me what the score was and winding Wilf and Bill up. At one stage I felt this whack up the back of my legs and there was Wilf frothing at the mouth on the other side of the net. I carried on playing for a few minutes then as the ball came to Wilf I stepped under the net and charged him with my shoulder. He flew across the gym and wrapped up against the radiator. Even that wasn't enough to silence Gilesy and as he walked up the corridor to the dressing-room he kept shouting out: 'What's the score. "H"?'

I would often give Johnny and some of the other lads a lift home after training. Even on the short journey to Talbot Road he'd be messing about. On one occasion I decided it was time to teach him a lesson. Johnny was in my car along with Derry lad Jimmy Shields. I drove up Warwick Road and turned right. Johnny said: 'You've gone the wrong way,' but I kept on driving. They were soon screaming at me to stop, but I carried on past the motorway. We were beyond Altrincham, about ten miles from Old Trafford, when I stopped. I told the two lads to get out. They complained they'd no money, so I put my hand in my pocket, threw them a penny each and drove off. I did attempt this prank again, this time with near-tragic consequences.

I was driving down the Chester Road towards Sale when the lad who was in the back with Gilesy told him to grab the car keys. To distract me he grabbed me around the neck, preventing me from getting to Johnny, and more importantly, telling them that the steering wheel locked when the keys were removed. Fortunately I had a cigarette in my hand and a couple of seconds of burning flesh later I was free to explain how close they'd come to getting us killed. Such shenanigans were commonplace. The key was not to overstep the mark and attract the unwanted attention of the boss.

Ten days after the FA Cup final we went on a tour to Italy which included matches against Juventus and a Roma Select. The team was gathered in a hotel bar in Livorno. The Cup final lads were downing pints and singing songs – Nobby Stiles, Shay Brennan and myself were drowning our sorrows after missing out on a place in the squad at Wembley. I wasn't much of a drinker in those days but I took a sherry to be sociable. Johnny Giles, who was just a kid, joked: 'Don't worry about not being in the first team. You may be reserves, but your time will come.' He repeated the taunt to Shay and Nobby before I warned him not to push his luck. John's timing wasn't the best, I mean I'd just missed out on a Cup winner's medal. Still he kept on mouthing and in mock anger I grabbed the sides of the chair. Gilesy thought I was serious and when one of the arms of the chair came away in my hand, he turned to Shay and said: 'Let's get the f—- out of here!'

Eventually, on the way to my room I heard Shay and Johnny laughing. I decided it was time for some payback. I repeatedly pushed at the wooden panel on their door; its creaking was accompanied by my muffled threats to get the two of them. Not happy with their frantic calls for me to piss off, I decided to give the door handle a kick. I'd obviously had a few glasses of sherry too many, though, and I missed the handle and my foot went straight through the door. I was jammed in the door as Johnny and Shay shouted about ringing for help and tried to make a barrier with the wardrobe. Things then went from bad to worse. In an effort to free my leg, the entire door pulled free, along with the door frame and part of the wall. I quickly left the scene of the crime and returned to the room I was sharing with Nobby Stiles. I composed myself for a couple of minutes and then casually walked out of the room and peered around the corner. Jimmy Nicholson, the young Northern Ireland international, was staggering down the corridor more than a little worse for wear. He stopped and just stared at the damage to the door, so I nonchalantly walked around the corner and said: 'Jimmy, did you do that?' The poor lad didn't know what was happening, so I grabbed him by the arm, took him to his room, and put him to bed.

I returned to my room, stripped down to my underpants and climbed under the covers. Before too long I heard voices coming from the corridor. I sneaked out for a look and there was Matt Busby, Jimmy Murphy, Jack Crompton, the hotel manager and the house detective, all marching towards Johnny and Shay's room. I ran back to my room, dived into bed. Nobby was flapping, asking what was going on, and I told him to mind his own business and say I'm asleep. There was a knock at the door. It was Matt. Nobby feigned drowsiness when he answered and was told to open the door. I was shaking like a leaf. The lights went on and Matt pulled back my covers. 'What's going on?' I asked with mock surprise. 'Don't give me what's going on! There are bits of door and wall lying all over the place out there. There's only one man capable of doing that.' Matt then threatened that we'd all be heading to Manchester first thing in the morning if the culprit didn't own up. The following morning the door and wall had been patched up. Nothing more was said about the matter, but Gilesy said he knew it was me. He'd recognised the laughter.

Paddy Crerand was another who came to the fore in the early 1960s. Like any new recruit Pat knew very few people when he first arrived at United in 1962. Paddy wasn't one for airs and graces. He was what you might call earthy, a real product of his upbringing on the tough streets of Glasgow. I recall when we played Manchester City in what was an annual fixture to raise funds for the Duke of Edinburgh Playing Field Awards. After the match all the players attended a function with his Royal Highness at the City Hall. I was standing with Noel Cantwell, Denis Law and the Duke of Edinburgh. There we were, a Northern Irishman, a southern Irishman and a Scot, prattling away about polo of all things. Who should appear with his hands in his pockets but Paddy Crerand. Noel stepped out and performed the introductions: 'Your Royal Highness, this is our wing-half, Pat Crerand.' The Duke said how pleased he was to meet Pat, who replied: 'How ya doing, Jimmy!' Not content with that slice of informality, he asked whether the Duke had been stationed in Derry during the war. His Royal Highness said: 'As a matter of fact I was,' and Paddy added: 'I know a couple of birds you were out wae.'

Paddy was not one to stand on ceremony. We'd been drawn in the European Cup against East Berlin side Vorwaerts and Matt Busby had warned us several times not to be mucking about because they had a different take on things. We flew to West Berlin and the following day went to Checkpoint Charlie to cross into the eastern sector of the city. We were taken into a room, a holding area, where each of us was handed three forms to fill in, two yellow and one green. Once again the boss reminded us that no one was to act the clown. We moved down to the first window, handed in the completed forms, then on to the second window, where one was returned. About half of our party had gone through when there was a shout: 'Halt, Crerand!' Two hours later we were still there. Paddy had filled in the surname on one of the forms as 'Bond'. Christian name: 'James'. Destination: 'Moscow'. Occupation: 'Espionage'.

Pat just couldn't help himself. If we were in the best seats in a theatre he'd be annoying the rows in front with his crinkling sweet wrappers. Then if the bloke in front turned around Pat would suggest a little off-the-cuff plastic surgery courtesy of the sole of his shoe. One night in a Southport Hotel he decided to order some food from room service. It was the early hours of the morning and we were playing cards on the bed. When the night porter came in Pat tried to enlist his co-operation with a not-so-subtle rattling of the change he'd placed in a drawer. The porter eventually returned with a plate of turkey and ham sandwiches and as he lingered near the door, Pat asked did he want a tip. The porter replied: 'Thank you, sir'. Pat said: 'Don't put black polish on brown shoes.' I gave him some stick for that, but he justified his actions by saying his mother back in Scotland worked from dawn to dusk for two and six. At one stage Bobby Charlton invited Pat and his wife Noreen out for a meal. What concerned Bobby, though, was if some waiter spilled something in Pat's lap. Bob was terrified he would chin him.

I also soon learned that Pat and my compatriot George Best had something in common. Neither experienced pre-match nerves. One game was much like the other for Paddy. At Wembley in 1963 the boss was furious when he wasn't in the dressing-room for the pre-match talk. Eventually, he sauntered in. Paddy had been listening to 'Abide With Me' and singing along with the fans. Having been told that it was a special moment at Cup finals, he wanted to experience it for himself.

As a player, Pat was something of an enigma. He wasn't blessed with pace, in fact, that's an understatement. Even at 35 I could run backwards quicker than Pat could sprint. In that respect Pat was similar to a player I watched on United's behalf many years later – Ronnie Whelan. Ronnie was no greyhound but, like Pat, he had a wonderful ability to make up for any deficiency in the pace department with his reading of the game. Sadly, United didn't heed my advice to sign him and Liverpool snapped him up. Despite Pat's lack of speed, the fact that he hardly ever headed a ball, and a meagre return of 15 goals in 392 games for United, he more than compensated for any failings. Speed of thought, vision and sublime passing were his forte. As for the lack of goals, well, his role became that of provider. Pat Crerand may not have been the most graceful athlete to ever lace a pair of boots, but I can't think of too many players who were any more effective.

Matt Busby would often make senior players room with the younger lads, or players new to the club. I think he was hoping I would bring a calming influence. Looking back, it was a privilege to have such a responsibility, to be able to help in some small way with the development of a player at Old Trafford. One player to benefit from me keeping an eye on his progress was Nobby Stiles.

We were travelling by train to Edinburgh for the match under the floodlights with Hibernian. The Hibs team had an English-born player called Joe Baker, whom United were rumoured to be interested in signing. Joe never did play for United, but he carved out a great career for himself. He went on to play with Denis Law in Italy, and also with Arsenal, Nottingham Forest and Sunderland. It was common practice at the time for a young apprentice to help with the kit at games. It was a way of blooding them, of introducing them to life with the first team. The boy who came with us to Easter Road was Norbert Stiles.

During the journey a few of the lads played cards. Nobby was getting terrible stick from some of the team, who were calling him Blind Pugh. On closer inspection I could see why. Nobby was practically balancing the cards on his nose. Later, I pulled him to one side and asked if he had been acting the fool or if he had bad eyesight. At first he said his eyes were fine, then he confessed he had a problem. He admitted having poor eyesight and that he stopped wearing glasses because of the slagging he used to get at school.

I was in the medical room having some treatment a few days later when Matt came in. I asked if he realised Nobby Stiles had bad eyesight, then recounted the story of the card playing. The boss sent for Nobby straight away. He denied everything, as any kid would when his shortcomings are being aired. Matt instructed Ted Dalton to send an optician and it turned out Nobby could hardly see his hand in front of his face. To this day he's lost without his glasses. Nobby overcame his poor eyesight by using contact lenses. Far less advanced than modern lenses, they would irritate enormously. After a match, when Nobby would take them out, he would resemble an alien from outer space, his eyes bloodshot and swollen. Much was made over the years about Nobby's appearance. One of Nobby's reserve team buddies was Jimmy Nicholson. A well-built lad, Jimmy was unfairly burdened with the tag 'the new Duncan Edwards'. In truth, Jimmy's *strength* was not his strength, he actually preferred to steal the ball from the opposition players than to batter them into submission. Nobby Stiles suffered in the same way. He was pigeon-holed as the rugged wee man with the crunching tackle and gap-toothed snarl. People used to laugh when I said Nobby was the best player of the lot, they just saw a thug.

Nobby Stiles, or Happy, as all the lads called him, is one of the most underrated players ever to play for Manchester United or England. He had a fantastic football brain. He would drop in beside Bill Foulkes at centre-half when necessary, the result of natural positional sense. The public? Well, they are always lured by the more overtly skilful players.

I suppose, looking back, I owe Nobby an apology. I used to wind the poor lad up something terrible. During the stay in Livorno we discovered there was an armadillo running around the hotel. A few of the lads threw an empty suitcase on top of it and then jumped up and down on it. This brush with the local wildlife did have one or two on edge, however, and poor Nobby was ready for the hills by the time I'd finished with him. I smuggled a lobster out of the restaurant and up to our room. I set it under the bed whilst Nobby took out his contact lenses and got ready for bed. I then switched off the main light, my bedside lamp, and told him to hurry up because I was exhausted. Over and over Nobby kept asking me to swear on my mother's life that I wasn't going to fool around, before finally getting into bed. He reached around to switch off his lamp and I quickly slipped the lobster under his covers. Seconds later there was this almighty scream. I switched on the light to find Nobby pinned against the far wall, screaming about something biting him and swearing that he'd never room with me again. A cruel trick, I know, but it still makes me laugh today.

Although the policy was still to develop players from within, United did make use of the cheque book to bolster the squad in the early 1960s. Prior to Denis Law's arrival, the board had splashed out on Noel Cantwell, a recruit from West Ham United, and Maurice Setters, a £30,000 acquisition from West Bromwich Albion.

Noel, from Cork, was how you imagined a footballer to be. Tall, with a fine physique, he had few shortcomings. His biggest problem was adjusting to a different regime at Old Trafford. He was a product of Upton Park's Academy, where there was a more structured policy on coaching and formations. I remember we were travelling to Blackpool on the bus and he asked Matt what formation he planned to adopt and how he wanted him to play. The boss basically let him know he'd been signed for his ability and that his job was to go out and play. That's the way it was at United, you were given the freedom to go out and demonstrate that you were the best player in that position and deserved the right to wear the red shirt. Noel did find his feet. He became a fine player and a fine leader. Always articulate, always personable, he was a great asset.

Maurice Setters was one of the best defenders I ever played with. His problems arose when he developed delusions of grandeur. Occasionally Maurice would attempt to hit killer passes, or to make sorties into the opposition half. It wasn't his game. Maurice used to complain bitterly if these unsuccessful attempts at turning creator resulted in him being dropped, and his pals used to agree. I used to tell him: 'If you went over the halfway line I'd drop you too.' His game was not about spraying passes, he was a stopper. When he stuck to what he did best, he was a match for anyone. One of the most devastating tacklers I've ever seen, he was also a superb header of the ball for a small man.

For every Law, Crerand and Stiles, there were lads who failed to make the grade at Old Trafford. For some, it was a lack of ability, for others the inability to cope with the pressures associated with being part of the biggest club in the world. Albert Quixall falls into the latter category. He was deservedly called the golden boy of British football when he joined us from Sheffield Wednesday. A superb player, with an abundance of skill, there was little doubt he was a class act. Albert, though, became living proof that Manchester United is not the right club for everyone. As results went against us, he lost confidence. He became increasingly more introspective and despite playing 183 games and scoring 56 goals, Albert never managed to cope with the pressure cooker that is Old Trafford.

The youth team in the early '60s was also a breeding ground for talent and even these kids managed to attract upwards of 30,000 people to some of their games. Over the years it was fascinating to watch as they developed their own niche in the game. Two of George Best's contemporaries in the youth set-up were Eamon Dunphy and Barry Fry. Eamon has certainly made a name for himself, not least for his outspoken views over Roy Keane and the Republic of Ireland during the last World Cup. And I can tell you that *Dunph* was every bit as opinionated as a 15-year-old at Old Trafford.

We were playing at the back of the Stretford End one day and I caught him with a bad tackle. He picked himself up and threatened to go and see a solicitor. I'd never heard anything like it in my life, this coming from a scrawny-looking youngster. Even as a 15- and 16-year-old Eamon Dunphy spoke his mind. And he could play a bit too. Perhaps what held him back at United was his physique. He was a great athlete. In cross-country at the Ship Canal he could run all day. He had the lungs of a marathon runner, he was passionate about the game, but wasn't blessed with great physical attributes. Even so, Eamon did enjoy a good career, particularly with Millwall, before returning to Ireland.

I have to admit we've had our rows over the years, but I still enjoy seeing him spice things up. He has a wonderfully agile mind, although occasionally it appears to be a little too steeped in vitriol. A lot of other people do agree with many of the things he says, they just don't have the balls to speak out. At least Eamon Dunphy has the courage of his convictions.

Barry Fry, who joined United along with Dunphy in 1960, was just a smaller version of what you see today – a real jack the lad. He was a skilful ball player, although, like Eamon, he lacked a physical presence (not something you could level at Barry today). During the Northern Ireland Milk Cup youth tournament in 2002 I met up with one of Barry's former teammates, Jimmy Ryan. Jimmy was looking after one of the United teams and as we were chatting outside the changing-rooms at Coleraine Showgrounds some of the kids came out for a warm-up. I directed one young fellah to the training pitch and when I turned back, Jimmy asked: 'Do you know who that is?' It was Barry Fry's son. It's good to see the next generation coming through, and, like his dad, he's a skilful player.

I always felt a genuine bond with the young players whose tenure at Old Trafford coincided with mine. During my time as a senior pro I like to think I developed a rapport with many of them. Although these youngsters enjoyed varying degrees of success they form part of the fabric of United during the era after Munich. When I reminisce they also occupy equal billing with Bestie, Law and Charlton. Many of them slipped into relative obscurity, our paths crossing only at the occasional Old Boys' reunions. When I do attend these functions, though, it's men like Jimmy Elms, Frankie Haydock, John Connaughton, Carlo Sartori, Bobby Harrop and John Fitzpatrick whom I look forward to seeing. Some of them are bald-headed old men now, but they'll always be kids to me.

X

A KID FROM BACK HOME

Every Christmas, Easter, and summer holidays they came to try their luck. Hundreds of pimply faced youngsters with the shared dream of playing football for Manchester United. The most promising lads from across the British Isles were invited to The Cliff for trials – and I was about to be embarrassed by probably the smallest, scrawniest one of the lot. He was a painfully shy lad from the streets of Belfast who found expression with the ball at his feet. His name was George Best.

I'll never forget that first meeting. Frustrated by my lengthy rehabilitation from injury, I asked to join Johnny Aston Snr and his young lads for five-a-sides. It was a fairly unusual request as first-team players seldom had any contact with the trialists. At this point in my career I had played against many of the world's leading players, looking into the whites of their eyes as they bore down on my goal. Suffice to say I didn't anticipate too many problems during this kickabout with the kids.

I wasn't in goals long when this slip of a lad with short-cropped, raven hair broke through. Now I had a technique for these one-on-one situations, a method which had proved highly successful in club, European, and international matches. As the player neared and looked up, I feinted one direction, then went the other. It was a case of throwing a dummy before they did it to you. On this occasion, though, normal rules didn't apply. I was sold a dummy all right, and George ghosted past. I picked myself up, shrugged my shoulders and put it down to ring rust after my lay-off. A little later he wriggled clear again. I called his bluff and got the same result, a humiliating trip to *terra firma*. When George had the audacity to beat me a third time I got up and joked: 'You do that again and I'll break your bloody neck, son!' I had a good laugh and a chat with George and the other lads. But when I left, the image of this pencil-thin lad with the breathtaking skills lingered on.

Later that day I ran across Matt Busby at Old Trafford. He asked how I was getting on and I gave him my stock reply: 'Not bad, boss.' We chatted briefly and as he turned to walk away I asked if he'd seen the youngster, the little Belfast lad. He hadn't, and I suggested he take a look. A few days later we met again. 'I know the boy you mean. It's a pity he's so small,' he said. To his dying day Matt stood by the assertion that George was too small. In all truthfulness, he was.

A few months later, on one of his trips to Manchester, George introduced me to his father. Like any concerned dad, Mr Best asked me whether I thought his lad would get a contract. I assured him he would, even if that was not the consensus around Old Trafford at the time. George and his contract cropped up whenever Dick and I met after that. As a player I wasn't in a position to influence the club's decision, but when asked for advice I did suggest that he should insist on being there if George was indeed asked to put pen to paper.

United reached the FA Cup final in 1963, an opportunity for the club, and me, to banish memories of Nat Lofthouse and defeat by Bolton Wanderers five years earlier. I'd picked up a knock and missed some league games, but I was fully recovered in time for the final. Shay Brennan, Nobby Stiles and myself had played in every round, yet the three of us were left kicking our heels on the Wembley sidelines. Matt had decided not to change a winning line-up and we were not the best of company as our teammates celebrated the win over Leicester City at the post-match banquet. I was sitting with the first team when George came to the table and asked could his dad come over and have a word with me. I replied: 'No, son. But I'll come over to your dad's table.' George's mum was also there, plus some of the other youth players. Mr Best reminded me of the advice I'd given him over his son's contract. He added that Matt had agreed he could be there when the contract was signed. Unfortunately, it hadn't worked out that way. Dick Best only arrived in England on Cup final morning and George signed three days before. Once again he asked my advice. To be honest I wasn't in a particularly good mood, but I told him that if there was a misunderstanding he should remind Matt of his promise. Dick tried, unsuccessfully, to talk to Matt Busby that night. The following day he tailed the official party to the railway station. Spotting Matt and Jimmy Murphy standing on the platform, he blagged his way past the ticket collector. He told Matt there was nowhere else to run. Jimmy Murphy attempted to intervene, but was quickly put in his place. Dick was wasting his breath, however. Matt's response was to turn on his heels and board the train. For the record, the club's contract was £5 per week for 40 weeks, with £200 to his parents in lieu of what George would have received had he been an apprentice at the Harland & Wolff shipyard.

George and I were close, something that didn't escape the notice of Matt Busby. He made the first team and I didn't have long to wait before I became the unofficial liaison officer between the boss and George – an integral part of Matt's man-management strategy. Normally when the boss called you into the referee's room it meant you were about to be dropped. He would ask how you thought you were playing and as a young lad you'd say: 'I could be doing better'. He'd then hit you with: 'Aye, you're right, I'll give you a rest.' As you got older and wiser you learned to be just as canny as Matt. An alternative answer was: 'Well, I played some games better than others.' If you were called into the medical room, however, it was because the boss wanted a chat or some advice. The first occasion I was called in for a chin-wag about George was 1964. He was only 17 at the time. Matt asked would I have a chat with my mate because he was running with a married woman who had left her husband and the press were chasing the story. He added that George was keeping company with some of the city's biggest gamblers (the boss said he knew them well because he'd run about with their grandparents) and had blown £100 in a single hand at blackjack in the Cromford Club. I left and joined the lads who were out running. I jogged up behind George and pulled him to one side. He said the affair with the married woman was over. Then he denied gambling at the Cromford. Lying was pointless, though, as Matt and the club's owner Paddy McGrath were best friends. I've always found it strange that so much has been made of George's womanising and drinking over the years because for me gambling was his biggest vice. No-one asked did he like a flutter?

I have no desire to continue discussing George's much-chronicled, and often much-hyped, rock-star behaviour. From the first time I met him in '62, until I left in '67, he was always a pleasant, quiet, well-mannered young man. Whatever his problems were off the field, on it the *little fellah*, as Matt and I called him, could be sublime. When George was on song, he was blessed with greatness. He was ice cold and seemingly free from nerves – even on the big occasions. He had no fear, he could tackle as well as take people on, he was good in the air and there was a devilment about his play when required. Above all, he was supremely confident.

George produced some stunning performances. But there's little doubt in my mind of the moment he made the transformation from rising star to superstar. It was the European Cup quarter-final on 9 March, 1966, against Benfica at the Stadium Of Light. The Portuguese had contested four out of the previous five European Cup finals and, inspired by Eusebio, they were well-nigh unbeatable at home. We won 3-2 at Old Trafford, but no-one gave us much chance of making it past the second leg in Lisbon.

There were 75,000 passionate Portuguese packed into the Stadium Of Light that night, each hellbent on unsettling the visitors from England. To make matters worse, our arrival on to the pitch was hampered by Benfica's attempts to gain a psychological edge, and by what you might call a changing room *bust-up*. A bell rang to tell us it was time to go out and we filed into the tunnel area. Unfortunately we were left standing for 20 minutes. Eventually, and with everyone just a little edgier than before, we had no option but to return to the dressing-room. Pat Crerand started playing *keepy-uppy*. Unfortunately, he lost control of the ball. The entire length of one wall was covered by a huge mirror and it suddenly exploded, shattering into a thousand pieces. It's funny now when I think about it, but poor Paddy was not the most popular chap at that precise moment in time, especially among the more superstitious players like Denis Law and myself who felt there was now no point in even going out on to the pitch.

As it happened, luck didn't have any bearing on that particular 90 minutes. We were 3-0 up at half-time and during the break Pat asked was there any chance we could get him another mirror. We eventually thrashed Benfica 5-1. It was a mesmerising team performance and a virtuoso display by George. He scored twice, his second a breathtaking solo effort where he rounded the keeper as effortlessly as that day he skinned me at The Cliff. There has been a lot of nonsense written over the years that Matt instructed us to keep it tight for the first 20 minutes and that George wasn't listening. That's absolute rubbish. Matt Busby never asked any team I ever played in to go out and defend. One of those who had quite literally written us off was Desmond Hackett from the *Daily Express*. He'd said that he would eat his trademark trilby if we won. At the post-match banquet who should be there but Desmond. We went down, tapped him on the shoulder, stood back and enjoyed his floundering.

George's performance in the Stadium of Light may have caught the attention of every press man in the country, but his fate was sealed by a decision on the flight home. The mood in our camp was understandably upbeat as we winged our way home and George started walking up and down the aisle wearing this huge sombrero he'd bought. The lads were egging him on and I shouted: 'Hey, Bestie, get that off.' Everyone else told me to leave the lad alone, but I tried to make the point that great players didn't need gimmicks. When we landed in England the press had a field day with two-goal George and his *hat* trick. The scribes dubbed him 'El Beatle' and from that day on his life became a goldfish bowl. There were many occasions when I felt George's teammates were often his worst enemy. There was nothing deliberate, or malicious, but they seemed incapable of realising the need to protect George from the fame that was engulfing him.

There were times when Bestie chose to heed the wrong advice. I remember when he was troubled with a knee injury before the first leg of the European Cup semi-final against Partizan Belgrade. We lost the match 2–0. I didn't do well in that game, few did, with Dennis Law having a particular nightmare. George, even with his gammy leg, was our most effective player. That was until 13 minutes from time when he was forced out with a recurrence of his knee injury. We played Arsenal between the European legs. In the dressing-room before the match Matt was pacing up and down. He said nothing, which was his norm pre-match. I asked him where the *little fellah* was? Matt said he'd allowed him home to see his parents before returning to have a cartilage operation at St Joseph's Hospital the following morning. Later in the week I was asked to go to the medical room. Matt quietly asked had I seen George. I said: 'No, is he not in hospital?' In fact, George had only arrived back in Manchester that morning saying his knee was okay. He had been to see a man in Belfast who had supposedly cured the problem. Matt said: 'For God's sake, go and have a word with him.'

At that time we were training at the Ship Canal Ground, an unpopular venue with most of the lads because there was too much damn room to run around. I jumped in my little Renault Dauphin, drove to training and ran a couple of laps so I could catch up with George. I asked where he had been and he said his dad had taken him to see a man who'd sorted things. I told him he'd had the finest medical opinion and had chosen instead to see some man in Belfast. I said: 'You're mad,' and asked what he looked like. I asked was he as tall as me, if he wore a long white sheet and if he had a crown perched on his head? Bestie accused me of losing the plot, but I said he was the only madman because it must have been Jesus himself if he'd been cured by a laying-on of hands. Within half an hour of our chat, George's knee locked up whilst he was jogging. He ended up in hospital where he had his cartilage removed and suffered the further complication of a clot.

Impressionable – yes; foolish – most certainly; but George could also be generous to a fault. At the height of his powers he became the poster boy of the Swinging '60s. He had the women, the flash cars and clothes to match. He was a star whose stock was soaring. It was enough to send anyone off the rails, but there were always glimpses of the George I knew before Benfica. I recall one occasion when he arrived at the training ground in his Sunbeam Alpine, the back of the car crammed with jackets and shirts from his boutique. He carried in the clothes, threw them down on a table in the dressing-room, and told the young apprentices to help themselves. Some of the staff dived in first.

I left Manchester United in 1967. After a brief spell at Stoke City, I went into football management with Shrewsbury Town. I worked alongside Jimmy McLaughlin, a dear friend and the most successful manager in League of Ireland history. The two of us moved on to Swansea City in the early '70s. George had walked out of Old Trafford for the first time on New Year's Day, 1974. Jimmy and I were in the office at Vetch Field when Jimmy said: 'Do you know, "H", you're the only person George would come back to play for.' Now Swansea City was a club with its own problems at the time. We were trying to rebuild and I knew bringing George to Wales would be a tremendous boost for everyone concerned, not least George. I rang Matt Busby at King's Road, Stretford, to wish him a Happy New Year and to enquire how he was. 'I was like a lion last night, but I'm like a lamb this morning,' was his reply. It was what the boss always said after he'd had a rough night. We talked on and I asked him would he like to see the *little fellah* back in football. I suggested that George come to Swansea for a month, an opportunity to dispel this public image as a troublemaker. After that, even if he didn't want to return to United, he could be sold. The boss, who was acting as a director at Old Trafford, liked the idea. He thought it best, though, if I spoke to the manager, Tommy Docherty. I arranged to meet George on a couple of Sundays to discuss it. Eventually he agreed and my parting words were: 'Don't you let me down, boy!'

I tried repeatedly to contact Tommy Docherty. He'd been messing about over the signing of a prodigy of mine at Shrewsbury, Jim Holton. The Doc said he would sign him, then let the lad down. He knew I wasn't happy about the way he'd been treating Jim, so, needless to say, I was the last person he wanted to meet. Finally, I asked my wife Carolyn to phone the club as an everyday punter and find out when, and where, the first team would be training. It was two o'clock at The Cliff and I telephoned Ron Crowther at the *Daily Mail*. I'd known Ron from the time he worked at the *Yorkshire Post* and I was playing for Doncaster. I trusted him and asked would he meet me outside the gates of The Cliff. The first person I ran across was groundsman Dave Royle (his brother Joe fulfilled the same role at Old Trafford) and he jokingly asked was I here for the manager's job. I asked where Tommy

Docherty was and told Dave not to go and get him because if he was forewarned he'd scarper. I walked up the stairs to the staff room, knocked the door and walked in. There was the Doc, Laurie Brown, Bill Foulkes and Pat Crerand. Paddy starting nattering to me, but Tommy grabbed my arm and took me into his office. Paddy tried to follow me in, but the Doc told him firmly to clear off. Straight away Tommy was on the defensive. 'Look, ham and eggs–' he always called me that '–I'm gonna sign the big man, I'm gonna sign him.' It was clear he thought I was there to slate him over his handling of Jim Holton. I said: 'That's not what I'm here for, I'm here about George Best.' Docherty pointed out of his office window to the training pitch below and what he said about George I wouldn't like to repeat. Suffice to say that he was not Bestie's number one fan.

I explained my plan to take him on loan to Swansea for a month. Docherty said he'd agree as long as George returned to training for a week. I knew that was a total non-starter. I said: 'You know I've a reputation for being stubborn, well I'm not in the same league as George.' I knew George would never back down and we finally reached the compromise that he could come to Swansea if he returned to United for one day. I met Ron Crowther at the gates as planned and together we drove to Deansgate, where George had taken over the former British Airways offices. I'd arranged to meet George, but there was no sign of him. Ron was worried George would not speak to him – he wasn't exactly a fan of the press at the time. So I went in to wait for George, whilst the northern sports editor of the *Daily Mail* waited outside like a naughty schoolboy at the door of the headmaster's study. George arrived in his white Rolls-Royce – you could hardly even see him behind the steering wheel. I told George that Ron was outside, convincing him that a press ally was essential. How right I was.

Bestie did the piece with Ron, then I phoned Pat Crerand and asked him what the deal was with Tommy Docherty. I knew Pat would have already spoken to the Doc, so as he confirmed the agreement about one day at United and a loan move to Swansea I held out the phone so Ron could hear. I asked Pat where the Doc was, then I phoned the Piccadilly, paged him and once again held the phone out so Ron could hear it from the horse's mouth.

After I'd said my goodbyes to Ron and George I travelled home to Shrewsbury (where we were still living) for a night's sleep. I was up early, drove over the mountains to Wales and stopped off in Abergavenny at about 6 a.m. for breakfast. I bought the *Daily Mail* and the back page lead was George saying the only man he'd play for was Harry Gregg and that he had agreed a one-month loan period at the Vetch Field. That same night in the *Manchester Evening News* a story about Bestie was also making the headlines: 'Best for Swansea – Sick Joke' by Tommy Docherty. A week later I received a call from one of George's best friends, Malcolm Wagner. He told me Bestie wouldn't be coming to Swansea. I said: 'Tell him from me that I won't accept that 'til the day I die unless he tells me to my face.'

Jim Holton eventually did join Manchester United and the chant of 'Six foot two, eyes of blue, big Jim Holton's after you' became a favourite of the Stretford End. I went up to Old Trafford to see him play. George was back in the fold by this stage and in the players' lounge (which used to be our gymnasium) after the game I'm standing chatting to Jim and who should walk in but Bestie. I hadn't spoken to him since he let me down. I said to Jim: 'Look who's here!' Jim said: 'Don't start, boss.' I assured him I wouldn't. Eventually, Bestie left his entourage and came over. He stood there like a wounded puppy and I asked: 'Why didn't you ring me yourself?' He answered: 'I couldn't, "H", I just couldn't.' I told him he was a little prat and he asked was that all I had to say. He then said: 'Can I go now?' I said yes and he went back to his mates. George walked over to one of the men in his party and I saw him ask George who I was. Seconds later he came over and bawled out: 'How ya doing, big man!' I said: 'Are you speaking to me?' He added: 'How are you, big man? It's the way I tell 'em.' It was the comedian Frank Carson. Here was someone who had to ask who I was, then wanted to come over and act like he knew me to be Mr Big Time. I told him to piss off back to his company.

I honestly wasn't annoyed at George, he didn't owe me anything. But I suppose I did feel a little let down. What really hurt, though, was to watch his (and United's) downward spiral, the final departure from Old Trafford, the descent into drink and gambling, the twisted personal life. But when he went to the League of Ireland and still couldn't hack it, I became concerned that something was seriously wrong. I was manager at Crewe Alexandra and after dropping off the kids at school one morning I sat down in the office to read the papers. There was a story about Cork City freeing George Best after only the third week. I had known George since his arrival at United. I'd watched him develop into a world-class footballer. I couldn't believe things had come to this. I took a chance and rang Mrs Fullaway's, George's old digs when he was at United. Now, here's all this talk of George Best the superstar, the lothario and legendary drinker. And yet, where do I find him? Back in the safe environment of that humble house in Chorlton, a sanctuary from the pressures of fame. I just couldn't accept that George couldn't cut it at Cork. In fact, I was now so convinced he must be ill that I asked whether it was cancer or TB. Perhaps I just didn't want to accept his fall from grace was related to his complicated personal life and problems with alcohol. George told me he just had a cold and that he'd arranged to play a few matches for Freddie Pye at Stockport County before heading to America.

Months later I received a transatlantic call. George had spoken to his current employers and they were sounding me out about becoming manager. Not long after, George and his new American teammates came over to England and played a match at Brentford. I was invited and sat in the Directors' box. It was an embarrassing experience. I watched George come out on to the pitch and he looked like a completely different person to the one I remembered. He never once straightened his right leg and was clearly struggling. His then wife Angie was sitting near me and she kept on about how it wasn't George's fault. She blamed the guys he was playing with, anyone and everything except George himself. The state George was in was just too much to bear. At half-time I got up, went over to Angie Best and asked her to tell George that I'd been there. Then I left and went home. That wasn't the George Best I knew.

We lost touch for a while and I eventually returned home to Ireland and bought the Windsor Hotel on the promenade in Portstewart. One day, out of the blue, I got a call from George asking me to come to his testimonial dinner at the Europa Hotel in Belfast. I put on the bib and tucker and went to the city. He had me placed at one of the circular top tables. Matt

Busby was there, as was the *Belfast Telegraph*'s chief soccer writer Malcolm Brodie, Eamon Dunphy, who'd played in the same team as George, and Michael Parkinson, whom I first met when he was a young journalist in Barnsley and I was with Doncaster Rovers. I wasn't there long when who should walk into the room but Shay Brennan. Tanned, handsome as ever, he looked a million dollars. Was this really the same man who had been so ill? When I was at Carlisle I was told by Johnny Giles that the Bomber was very sick. I'd called Shay up in Waterford and his wife Liz answered. I said: 'This is Father Gregg. Could I speak with Seamus?' This happy-go-lucky man I'd known came on the phone distraught. He had heart trouble and was due to go into hospital. I tried to cheer him up and he told me if he made it I'd be the first person he'd ring. I hadn't heard from him, or seen him, until that night when he walked into the Europa Hotel. It was great to see him looking so good.

Michael Parkinson, Malcolm Brodie and Eamon Dunphy spoke eloquently about Bestie that night. Eamon said that none of the young lads thought he would get a contract because he was so greedy and never passed the ball. He added that Harry Gregg found him and that Matt Busby allowed the flower to flourish. Then it was the turn of the man himself. George said before he attempted to make a speech he wanted to mention someone he respected more than anyone else because they were always honest with him. I was stunned when he said my name. I stood up, then quickly sat down again. I have to admit it was a touching gesture from George. What a wonderful evening it turned out to be. Not least because I knew then that George remembered and appreciated our friendship.

I would like to think that George and I trusted each other over the years. I tried to offer the best advice I could when we were together at Manchester United, and I'm proud to say that I played a part in him getting the first of his 37 international caps for Northern Ireland. Bertie Peacock was manager and I rang him to tell him about this kid at Old Trafford who was something special. Bertie and the Northern Ireland selectors included George for the match with Wales in 1964 without ever having seen him play.

What I've always refused to do, though, is jump on the George Best bandwagon. Especially now. It was early one morning when my wife came to tell me the newspapers had been on the phone. George was in hospital and could be dying. I told her if they rang again to say I wasn't in. I called his dad and we had a long chat. He gave me the hospital's number and a codeword. The first time George spoke it was like listening to that same shy youngster whom I'd met all those years before at The Cliff. He sounded scared and vulnerable. It might appear a little insensitive, but in my own way I tried to lift the mood. I told George that he couldn't snuff it because I couldn't afford a wreath. And when he told me that even his backside was sore, I said: 'Just think of all the full-backs you gave a sore backside to.' We spoke virtually every day for the time he was in hospital.

In 2000 I was contacted by Patricia Diamond, a researcher for Ulster Television, to take part in a George Best tribute programme. It had been arranged before he went into hospital and George had agreed to take part. I asked her to run past me some of the names of the people who would be attending. Half of them didn't even know him and I decided there and then I wouldn't be going. Despite numerous follow-up calls I still didn't attend. I watched the programme at home and thought to myself: 'You were right, Gregg.' Hangers on, they constituted one of the biggest curses of George Best's life. George knows my feelings, he doesn't need me to go on television to broadcast it.

George was a well-mannered lad, an intelligent fellah, whose biggest problem was that he couldn't say no. If you phoned him up and asked him to play a match for you the following afternoon he'd say yes. Then if I called him up and said would he play for me at three o'clock the next day he'd say yes again. As for the drinking, I'm convinced it was a crutch. There are people can walk on a stage in front of hundreds of people and charm the birds from the trees. Yet, offstage they can be introverted. They need something to give them the courage to perform. George didn't need anything to run out at Wembley with a ball at his feet, but in the face of all the adulation he received in the early days I think he needed Dutch courage. It's not an excuse, but I think it's how he compensated for his shyness.

Sometimes I find it difficult to be in George's company now. It's upsetting. But the word tragedy should never be used by the media in connection with George Best. Tragedy is a death in the family, the loss of a loved one, not the decline of a once great sporting talent.

There's no doubt it's a shame that his lifestyle infringed on that rare gift he had to play football. He knows what I think on that subject, but then, that's how it is between George and me. There's no bullshit, no false sentimentality, just an honest relationship. Maybe he could have done with a few more of those in his life. But you'll have to ask him that.

In Dublin a couple of years ago we were having breakfast together following an after-dinner engagement the night before. We were sitting in a quiet corner and I asked him why he didn't show the world the *real* George Best. He asked what I meant. I told him he knew exactly what I meant. George paused, then looked at me and said: 'It's too late, Greggy. They see me as they want to see me.'

XI

RETURN TICKET

Without Shrewsbury Town, Swansea City and Crewe Alexandra there would have been no return ticket to Old Trafford. In the relative obscurity of Gay Meadow, The Vetch Field and Gresty Road I was given the opportunity to prove my worth as a coach and manager, to earn the right to return to my spiritual home.

Money was in short supply at Swansea, but Crewe took making a silk purse out of a sow's ear to a whole new level. When I arrived at the club they were preparing to apply for re-election to the Football League for the fourth year in succession. With confidence and coffers low, the job I had chosen to accept was nothing short of a mission impossible. Right from the start I made it clear to the players that they had something to be proud of, they were members of an exclusive club with only 92 members. I emphasised they were an English League club, not Crewe YMCA. For my part, I would do all I could to develop the team. At my previous clubs I'd been successful in nurturing young talent. I'd also derived great enjoyment from watching these young men go on to greater things. The transfer of Brian Parker from Crewe Alexandra to Arsenal, though, remains one of the most unusual deals I've ever been involved in.

My connection at Highbury was a gentleman called Gordon Clark, a former team-mate of Peter Doherty at Manchester City. Gordon was Bertie Mee's right-hand man and I'd helped him out with the signing of Jimmy Rimmer and Brian Kidd. Bearing in mind my track record, Arsenal let it be known that they were on the lookout for an understudy to Rimmer. Bob Wilson was retiring and with Jimmy established as the club's

No 1 they thought I might point them in the right direction. I had a lad called Geoff Crudgington at Crewe whom I thought might fit the bill and Bobby Campbell came along to watch him in action against Colchester. Geoff was perfect, a talented lad who was not overly ambitious and would have been content to play second fiddle to Jimmy at a club like Arsenal. Unfortunately for Geoff, he had a bit of a howler and despite my protestations, Arsenal cooled on any transfer. Crudgington may have come off their shopping list, but that didn't stop the Londoners pressing me for an alternative. Geoff would eventually sign for Swansea City, with whom he won a Second Division Championship. I had no option but to resort to plan 'B'. Enter big Brian Parker.

Now Brian was an unusual character. A giant of a lad from Wigan, he would not have been my first choice to put in the shop window. Nevertheless, Crewe desperately needed the money and if I could sell him to Arsenal then so be it. Unfortunately, Brian wasn't playing ball. I attempted to throw him in for the final league match of the season against Graham Taylor's Lincoln City. I thought it would be an opportunity to let Arsenal take a look at him, but Brian said his wife was expecting him home for tea that evening. Yes, I know it's hard to believe, but that's what he told me. I'd already taken Geoff aside and explained that he wasn't being dropped, but that I had a good reason for playing Brian Parker. Now I had to call him back and tell him he was playing again. However, thanks to my part in the sale of Rimmer and Kidd, Arsenal agreed to play a friendly at Gresty Road. Geoff played in the first-half, but I decided to gamble and send Brian on for the second. He was only on the pitch a few minutes when he made a great save. The dug-outs at Gresty are partially below pitch level and the next thing I know there's someone tugging at my arm. Bobby Campbell, dressed in a suit, has crawled along the track from the Arsenal bench and is saying to me that they'll take Brian. Despite Bobby's unorthodox approach, and several attempts to talk to me after the match by, among others, Jimmy Rimmer and Brian Kidd, I didn't want to appear too keen. I told Arsenal to give me a call on Monday morning.

A subsequent meeting took place between Bertie Mee and myself in the Tickled Trout Hotel on the East Lancs Road and the following week he called to say that, subject to a medical, they would sign the lad. I told my coach, John Manning, to go over to the train station and when Brian Parker arrived from Wigan to keep him there. I rushed to the office, grabbed a float from the secretary and took Brian to London. As he took his medical I walked nervously around Highbury, worrying that something would go wrong at the last minute to wreck the deal. That evening there was a Board meeting at Crewe. They, incidentally, were totally in the dark over Brian's move south. I told them I had sold a player. They didn't take me seriously at first, then, realising I wasn't joking, enquired as to who the individual was. I told them it was Brian Parker and that he was heading to Arsenal. A smile broke across the face of the chairman, a great character called Norman Rowlinson. 'Bloody hell, I think the manager's serious. Gentlemen, open the bar!' The postscript to this story is a phone call I received about a year and a half later from my compatriot Terry Neill. He had taken over at Arsenal from Bertie Mee and wanted to inform me that they were releasing Brian Parker. He was giving me first refusal. I'd just signed Drew Brand from Everton, so I declined. Brian ended up playing the rest of his career at Yeovil Town.

Things went well for me at Crewe. We never again had to apply for re-election and the bank balance, which had been permanently red, eventually turned black. I was happy there, but when the manager's job became vacant at Stoke City I decided to apply. It wasn't that I was desperate to leave, but it presented an opportunity to ply my trade in the First Division. It was around this time that I arrived for work to find a message asking me to ring Dave Sexton at his home in Alderley Edge. I phoned and he asked if I would be interested in coming back to Old Trafford.

I'd known Dave since my days at Swansea. Over dinner he asked did I think the boy I'd sold to Villa (John Phillips) could do a job as back-up to Peter Bonetti at Chelsea. I told Dave if he signed John it would be Peter who would end up as number two. John was only 17 when I handed him his first-team début and he remains the best goalkeeper of that age that I've ever worked with. He did indeed join Chelsea and won a Cup-Winners' Cup medal with them in 1971. John played in both legs of the

TOWERING PERFORMANCE: My second full cap for Northern Ireland was in the win over England at Wembley in 1957 (our first for 30 years). I'm deflecting the ball away from the on-rushing Tommy Taylor, with my teammate Jackie Blanchflower in close attendance. Sadly, Tommy lost his life at Munich, whilst Jackie never played again following the injuries he sustained in the crash.

THE BATTLE OF WINDSOR: Danny Blanchflower leads us out before a packed Windsor Park in what was originally scheduled as a World Cup qualifier against Italy (December, 1957). Unfortunately, the referee was fogbound and the match reduced to the status of friendly. It proved anything but and the match remains one of the most infamous in Irish soccer history. (Northern Ireland, from left: Danny Blanchflower, Jackie Blanchflower, me, Billy Bingham, Wilbur Cush, Jimmy McIlroy.)

GROUNDED: Fog prevented the referee from attending the World Cup qualifier with Italy, and I was its next victim. I missed the re-scheduled match because of fog at Manchester's Ringway Airport and, frustrated out of my mind, was forced to watch us reach the World Cup finals on television.

THE KING AND I: Being introduced to King Gustav of Sweden before the match with holders West Germany at the World Cup finals in 1958.

HERR GREGG: The match that played a major part in me being voted Best Goalkeeper at the 1958 World Cup finals. We drew 2–2 with the reigning World champions, West Germany. I'd damaged my ankle ligaments in the first few minutes of the game and, as you can see, Gerry Morgan heeded the plea to leave my boot on (I knew the ankle would swell and I'd have to go off) and strapped ankle, boot *et al*.

DOWN, BUT NOT OUT: I was told my damaged ankle would take eight weeks to heal and I missed the return match with Czechoslovakia. I was left kicking my heels on the sidelines, but when Norman Uprichard broke a bone in his hand against the Czechs I threw away the stick and played in the World Cup quarter-final against France.

PETER THE GREAT: Peter Doherty pictured back in Coleraine with the FA Cup he won with Derby County in 1946. Peter was an incredible player, coach and man. He has never received the credit he deserves, not least for what he achieved in guiding the minnows of Northern Ireland to the last eight of the 1958 World Cup

DENIS THE MENACE: I just got to the ball in the nick of time on this occasion. You had to be quick when Denis Law was about. Denis, seen here during his first spell with Manchester City, was a truly instinctive goalmouth predator.

UNITED: A photograph taken of the entire Old Trafford staff (season 1962–63). In the youth team on the right (eighth from right) is a young George Best. The two lads on his right are Eamon Dunphy and Barry Fry. The first team (seated from left) is Johnny Giles, Mark Pearson, Nobby Stiles, Bill Foulkes, Nobby Lawton, Albert Quixall, Bobby Charlton, Jack Crompton (Trainer/Coach), Maurice Setters, Matt Busby, Shay Brennan, me, Alex Dawson, Noel Cantwell, David Herd, Dennis Viollet

BESTIE: No wonder they called him the Fifth Beatle. Myself and a smiling George Best pictured at the height of his fame.

SCALING THE HEIGHTS: Before the Benfica match in Lisbon (March **1966**) which elevated George Best into the realms of football's first superstar. Matt Busby must already be aware of what a hot property George is about to become, judging by the close eye he's keeping here on his young star. (From left: John Connelly, Bobby Charlton, me, Pat Crerand, Matt Busby, George Best, David Herd, Nobby Stiles, Denis Law, Tony Dunne, Shay Brennan, Bill Foulkes.)

PUT TO THE SWORD: Maurice Setters (extreme right) and myself in the company of three of the greatest managers in the history of football. To my right are Matt Busby, Stan Cullis and Bill Shankly.

SPIRITUAL HOME: I returned to Old Trafford as coach (standing second from right) 17 years after leaving for Stoke City. This Manchester United squad photograph was taken prior to the start of the 1979–80 season. Dave Sexton (extreme left), like others, found his role as manager of United anything but easy.

THE GREGGS: The Gregg family pictured during my spell as manager of Crewe Alexandra. (From left: Julie, Karen, Carolyn with John, myself and Suzanne, Linda, Jane.) My family have always been so supportive during what was often a nomadic life as player and coach.

FORTY YEARS ON: In a touching letter UEFA invited the crash survivors back to Munich for the 1998 Champions League final between Borussia Dortmund and Juventus. We were also presented with these Bayern Munich shirts with our names emblazoned on the back. (The four survivors with shirts are from left: Ray Wood, Bill Foulkes, Jackie Blanchflower and me.) Sadly, both Jackie and Ray have since passed away.

semi-final against Manchester City before moving aside to let Peter Bonetti resume in goal for the final against Real Madrid.

I arranged to speak face-to-face with Dave and made it clear that I didn't see myself as a goalkeeping coach (that was the role he'd offered me at United), but as a coach . . . full stop. We discussed a few of the finer details and more than a decade after leaving Old Trafford I was on my way home. It was a strange feeling returning to United. When I'd joined as a player I hadn't been in awe of the club. Yet, that's exactly how I felt now.

The Manchester United I found on my return bore little resemblance to the one I remembered. Under Matt Busby the players were subordinate, now they seemed to possess the power. Maybe it was a product of the times, but I had difficulty relating to the new regime. It did not take long to realise that things had indeed changed, both on and off the field.

Tommy Docherty was sacked following his affair with Mary Brown, the wife of United's physio Laurie. It was the final straw for a club which could not excuse having its good name dragged through the gutter. Dave Sexton appeared to be the ideal choice – quiet, dependable and, perhaps most importantly, uncontroversial; he offered stability where before there had been volatility. Caution, though, has never been the United way. Of equal importance to delivering trophies is the flamboyance and excitement which characterised the great sides which had gone before. Sadly, for Dave, his failure to serve up a sufficient slice of style alongside workmanlike fare eventually cost him his job.

The Manchester United I had joined was in danger of drowning in a sea of mediocrity and the natives were growing increasingly restless. I recall watching us play Aston Villa in February 1979 at Old Trafford. Sammy McIlroy was brought down in the final minute and Jimmy Greenhoff's penalty helped us get out of jail. I could sense the unease in the crowd and with Dave Sexton's former club QPR due to visit the following Tuesday, I decided it was time to speak up. Dave Sexton's approach was gaining few friends on the terraces and the more I observed the harder it became to bite my tongue. I went home and told Carolyn that I was going to say something. I felt he deserved the same loyalty shown to me. She was not best pleased. We'd just bought a new house and Carolyn felt I should just keep my head down and get on with the job. She was probably right, but the following Monday I did indeed have my say.

It wasn't easy to speak my mind. I didn't want to appear out of place, but as far as I was concerned this was for Dave Sexton's benefit, not mine. I told Dave that in my experience there was no way the fans, or the board for that matter, were going to put up with the current situation indefinitely. I reminded him that United was expected to play with vitality, that failure to entertain was just as likely to lose him his job as poor results. Dave said he had been manager and coach at all his previous clubs, but at United the coach was Tommy Cavanagh. He walked over, shook my hand and thanked me for the advice. We led QPR 1–0 at half-time, yet the players were still booed off the pitch. At the end of 90 minutes United had doubled their tally, yet one woman hit Dave Sexton with her shoe as he walked back up the tunnel.

Clearly my coaching ethos differed markedly from many at the club. My friend and former team-mate Tommy Cavanagh is a case in point. Cav is a fiery, chest-thumping type of coach. That's his style and some respond to this technique. In one outburst he told a player: 'You're not fit to pick up your f——g wages!' Another was accused of being 'f——g brainless' and a third, an England international, was told: 'Tommy Docherty signed you, but I wouldn't have done.' When one of the players piped up that there were still 45 minutes to play, he was told to shut his mouth, that if he had his way he wouldn't be at the club either. Now, in my book, that is not the way to coach. I turned to Dave Sexton and mouthed: 'Can I speak?' He shook his head, so I stormed out of the dressing-room, nearly taking the door off its hinges in the process. After the match I took the opportunity to speak with the four players who had been on the receiving end of the half-time ear-bashing. I advised them that in the future they should not lower themselves to answer back, but merely say: 'I know I'm playing badly. Can you help me?' Invariably that leaves the person ranting with nothing left to say. Shouting and swearing can have its place, but I feel that criticism of players has at least to be constructive. For the record, the four players bawled out were Sammy McIlroy, Mickey Thomas, Steve Coppell and Ray Wilkins.

Tommy Cavanagh had his way of doing things, I had mine. Who's to say which of us is right? I mean, Cav could go through some players for a short cut and the same men would come and tell me it was just what they needed. And there's one thing about Cav, he never sat on the fence in his life. He said what he thought, and even if I cannot agree with his methods, I do admire that. Needless to say, though, our different styles of coaching did create some friction.

I'll never forget the day at training when Dave Sexton asked me if I would fill in at right-back for the second team. Dave always gave me a bit of stick for doing the same runs as the young players and at 47 I was still in good nick. To be honest I was chuffed to be asked. The rest of our defence was made up of a young centre-half called Kevin Moran, Steve Patterson, a converted centre-forward, and Stewart Houston. Facing me was Mickey Thomas, whom I'd known since his Wrexham days. Mickey would skin you alive if you dived into the tackle, but stand off and he didn't know what to do. Every time Mickey received the ball I closed him down and stepped inside. Mickey was almost pleading with me to tackle him and in the end he resorted to humping long balls which Paddy Roche collected with ease. Time and again we pushed out. With my back to Paddy I shouted to aim for the inside-right channel. Paddy had a very accurate drop-kick and sure enough he found Sammy McIlroy with a raking punt. Sammy chased it, moved in for the header past Gordon McQueen, but before the move could develop Cav shouted for the game to be stopped. He roared: 'There'll be no ale house football here,' before instructing Paddy to distribute the ball to his full-backs every time. They would then shuttle it across the back four. I said to Cav: 'I was always taught that good players see a picture and bad players don't. Therefore, you play what you see.' Tommy reiterated that every ball must be played across the back four. I told Cav that I had called the kick. I could feel my blood begin to boil, so rather than prolong the agony and say something I'd regret, I turned to Dave Sexton and asked his permission to go off.

If some of the players were fired up by Tommy's tirades, others reverted into their shell. Stevie Coppell was one who found it difficult. From starting out as a dashing winger, he was gradually getting more and more negative. It was obvious to me he was no longer enjoying his football. On a Saturday I would watch as he moved into the space occupied by right-back Jimmy Nicholl. He shouldn't have been back there, he was most effective in the attacking half of the pitch. All the time his head was down. He was going through a distinctly bad patch and yet no one seemed willing to lend a helping hand. You couldn't fault his application, in fact Steve would be at training every morning before the rest of the lads, doing a succession of sprints. But these great raking runs at top speed were merely another example of his problems on the pitch. He'd jog to level with the 18-yard line, then blast off hell for leather until he reached the other 18. All the time his head was down. Finally, I asked if he would object to me giving a bit of advice. I told Stevie to take a ball with him in the morning when he was doing his runs, to kick it, lift his head and then run. By knocking it, then lifting his head, he could see to make a pass. It was ultra-simple and yet I couldn't understand why no one else bothered to try to help a player make the most of his natural ability.

Of course, my primary role at United was to look after the club's goalkeepers. Gary Bailey was a lad who, I'm proud to say, flourished under my tutelage. I'd played against his dad, Roy, a fine keeper in his own right at Alf Ramsey's Ipswich Town. Gary, though, didn't always have it easy at United. Quite often he found himself at the mercy of the dressing-room wags, his clipped South African accent, Wits University schooling, and shock of blond hair singling him out for stick. As a goalkeeper, though, he had a lot going for him. He had a great physique, he was a good listener and he definitely wasn't short on self-belief. I recall one occasion when I had to bring him down a peg or two. He was getting just a little carried away and I reminded him that he owed his privileged position to Paddy Roche. Paddy, who incidentally was a far better keeper than most give him credit for, had the burden of following on from a terrace hero, Alex Stepney. He made it so much easier for Gary and I reminded him of that fact.

I will always be grateful to Dave Sexton for bringing me back to United. He was a likeable enough man, but I don't think he was the right man for the club. He loved United, of that there's no doubt, but I never felt he truly understood its ways. Take his abolition of the 'B' team. I heard about the plan from Paddy McGrath (a worry in itself because you'd expect to hear these things from inside the club) and I eventually confronted Martin Edwards over an informal cup of coffee. He confirmed it was going to happen and I told him that the 'A' and 'B' teams were the lifeblood of the club, the place where young players could be nurtured. Martin said that Dave had been told to make economies and this was one of the areas he had chosen to cut back. I suggested a far more sensible economy would have been to stop sending the first team to Mottram Hall on the Friday night before home games. Martin agreed, but the 'B' team still bit the dust. Dave axed the 'B' team as planned – two years later it was back.

To outsiders Manchester United's last season under Dave Sexton was not altogether unsuccessful. Second in the league to Liverpool was not bad by most standards. But then, United is not like other clubs. That was the very thing I tried to tell Dave a month after rejoining the club. In the end even seven straight wins wasn't enough to save him from the chop. The record books might suggest an impressive run of form, but a more telling statistic is that nearly 12,000 fewer fans watched Joe Jordan's winner in the 1–0 defeat of Norwich City than the brace he scored in the corresponding fixture the previous season. Still, I'd be lying if I said that Dave's sacking didn't come as something of a shock. After all, we were second in the league table to Liverpool. And it was not just the manager who found himself out of a job. When Ron Atkinson took over the axe also fell on Jack Crompton, Sid Owen . . . and me.

There had been no internal rumblings that Dave was about to get his P45. I'd gone to work as usual and when I got home Carolyn told me it had been on the news. After tea I rang Dave and he told me that when he'd arrived at the ground he had an idea something was amiss because the vultures were circling. Dave always had an uneasy relationship with the press. I carried on as usual and was somewhat surprised when Jack Crompton suggested I should apply for the job. I eventually took his advice and received a letter thanking me for my application. That was as close as I got.

I carried on working while the first team, under Jack Crompton's charge, flew to the Far East on tour. Martin Edwards approached me one morning and asked if he could have a chat. He wanted to pick my brains about candidates for the manager's job. I wasn't falling for that one, though, and said if he mentioned names, I, in turn, would give an opinion. There was no way I was going to start pulling names out of thin air. First up was Bobby Robson. I felt that Bobby might have been one of those men who was suited to, and successful at, one club. He had done brilliantly at Ipswich Town, but my gut feeling was that it is not always easy to reproduce the glory years at another club. He *was* Ipswich Town, which was not knocking him. Next was Lawrie McMenemy, who I'd spoken to informally about United, explaining the way things worked. I told him he might go off and secure Joe Jordan on a new contract, then go to the United board with the good news. That was the way Lawrie was used to dealing with such matters, but at Old Trafford they had a rigid wage structure and he might just find his good work undone. I got the distinct impression from our chat that he would not revel in United's methods of handling such matters. I told Edwards I didn't think he would come to Old Trafford. Billy McNeill was suggested, but I guarded against the dangerous combination of a young chairman (Edwards) and a young manager (McNeill). Next up was Ron Saunders. I knew Ron was a strict disciplinarian and I felt he was just the sort of man the club needed at that particular time. In my day the club kicked ass, driving players to become the best they could be. Now, I felt the club itself needed a good old-fashioned kick up the ass. Finally Ron Atkinson was mentioned. I told Martin Edwards that United was the Hollywood of football and it didn't need a John Wayne. I have to stress that all of these were my honest opinions at the time; there was nothing personal in them. A short time later I received a call from Jimmy Rimmer. He told me Ron Saunders was heading for United, at least that was the talk around Villa Park. Nothing more was said, no news about Dave Sexton's replacement filtering in my direction, and I left for a family holiday in Malta.

With two weeks of my break left I took a telephone call from Martin Edwards. He said he was sorry to be the bearer of bad news but Ron Atkinson had been appointed as manager and he didn't want me at the club. I was upset, as you can imagine, and told Edwards I was coming back to see him. He told me there was no point as he was heading off on his own holidays before I was due back in the country. He said I should speak to the manager. I reminded him that his father had been chairman when I returned as coach, so I would be coming back to speak to him. I queued up at 6.30 in the morning to get tickets back and cut the family's holiday short.

To be honest it didn't come as any surprise that Ron Atkinson wanted me out. We had history, stemming from my days in charge at Swansea City. Atkinson was adamant I'd sent a teenage Robbie James out to deliberately break his brother's leg in a match. Words were exchanged during and after the game. In recent years Atkinson repeated this nonsense in his book and let's just say the matter was settled out of court in my favour. Several of my players who witnessed my team talk, and events on the pitch, penned sworn affidavits which stated that I did not send anyone out to deliberately hurt an opponent. Quite the opposite, for I'd actually fined some of my own players in the past for foul play.

I arrived back in Manchester and went to Old Trafford. As I made my way to Martin Edwards' office I spotted a Mercedes parked outside with Ron Atkinson, his wife and daughter inside. I sat patiently outside the office and just as Martin Edwards opened the door, Atkinson and his family appeared through a door on the left. He shouted hello to me, but I just turned my back. Martin told Atkinson he'd only be a few minutes. My meeting was short and sweet. I was told that I was entitled to £2,200, but the club would bump it up to £4,200. I said to Martin: 'I've never been in a position like this before, so I'll have to go away and thing about it.' I added: 'By the way, that's two minutes.' As the Atkinsons passed me, I again turned my back. It was only when I returned home that I realised I was out of order. My gripe was with Ron Atkinson, not his wife and daughter. My own family did not want me to go, but I knew it was the right thing to do. I knocked on the door, went in and explained that it was not in my nature to hurt people who had done nothing to hurt me. I told Atkinson to pass on my apologies to his wife and daughter. He then started on about how big a man I was and that he wasn't getting rid of me because of our history, but because he wanted his own people. I stopped him in his tracks and said: 'You don't like me, I don't like you. I'm not going to wish you all the best. Goodbye.' Then I turned and left.

Eventually I returned to the club to arrange the final settlement. Martin Edwards had said in the press that United were going to look after their old hero Harry Gregg. I knew the outside world would think I'd got a small fortune from what Edwards had said and I went public in a newspaper to ensure there was no misunderstanding. I also made considerable changes to the club's statement. After deleting virtually every line I also insisted on a change from 'in full and total satisfaction' to 'in full and total payment'. From my point of view there was nothing satisfactory about the situation.

Setting aside my own disappointment, it was also a tough time for Jack Crompton and Sid Owen. Apart from a spell when Frank O'Farrell had been in charge, Crompo had been an ever-present at the club. A former club goalkeeper, trainer and coach, he was now shown the door. So too, Sid Owen, a man I have the utmost respect for. Youth team coach, Sid had an incredible way with young players. He was the man who had allowed the talents of Norman Whiteside and Mark Hughes to blossom. In fact, there are only two people whom I would have trusted with a youngster's formative football years. I would gladly have placed my own son in their charge. One is Sid Owen, the other a former Irish League player called Sammy McQuiston. I watched Sammy working with kids at Coleraine Showgrounds during a visit home and was incredibly impressed. Like Sid he pushed and cajoled the kids to develop their skills. It was not all about running and matches, but touch and control.

I suppose my departure gave Martin some sweet revenge for our run-in many years before, although I'm not suggesting for a moment that was the motivation. In fact, he probably doesn't even remember me having to cuff him around the ear as a 16-year-old for misbehaving in a hotel in Vienna during one of United's trips overseas. When I look back I'm not bitter about my Old Trafford exit. These things happen in life. I'm not saying it was easy, but if you go to church and they bring in a bad preacher, you don't fall out with the church. There isn't an individual who could ever shake my faith in the institution that is Manchester United.

XII

ROWS AND RECRIMINATION

Manchester United has become the club opposing fans love to hate. It has led to fortress Old Trafford and an *us* against *them* mentality. It wasn't always the case. Sure, there has been tribalism, that's part and parcel of a sport like football. But for every fan like the one at West Bromwich Albion who shouted at me: 'You should have died in '58!', there were hundreds who harboured a grudging admiration for what Matt Busby built. So what happened in the intervening years to incite such anti-United feeling? What caused this transformation?

The ageing process played its part. Thousands of supporters up and down the country who sympathised with United's plight post-Munich eventually gave way to a new generation. The new breed had only hand-me-down memories of Munich, no empathy for what United had been through, and merely saw the club as big, bold as brass and, occasionally, infuriatingly brilliant. But there was also another important factor. The way Manchester United conducted its business during the '70s and '80s saw a loss of respect, and not just in the blinkered eyes of opposing fans. The spirit that existed behind closed doors at Old Trafford during the Busby era had all but evaporated. Sure there were problems during Sir Matt's reign, but they were never aired in public. Post-Busby there was a deterioration in relationships, empires were built and good men fell by the wayside. Many of United's own followers were saddened by what they saw. I was one of them.

In 1970 Martin Edwards was made a director of Manchester United Football Club. It was part of a gentleman's agreement made on a trip with the youth team to Switzerland between Matt Busby, Louis Edwards and the rest of the board. The other part of this bargain, that Matt's son Sandy would also join the board, was never honoured. Initially there was a valid reason for Sandy's omission. Football League regulations prohibited anyone involved in bookmaking from being a director of a football club. However, by 1974 Sandy no longer had any connection with the bookies and dad decided it was time to act. On a club holiday to Majorca, Matt confronted his fellow board members. Alan Gibson didn't want to discuss the matter until Martin Edwards was present; Bill Young harboured reservations about Sandy (formerly a young professional with Blackburn Rovers) because of his friendship with the players; and Louis Edwards, supposedly Matt's friend, failed to offer his support. He told Matt it would be discussed at the next meeting of the board. At least that promise was kept, although the outcome was no more favourable. Sandy Busby would not be joining the board.

Louis and Martin may have got their way in this particular power struggle, but to this day Martin is involved in an on-going battle to establish any credibility as keeper of the United tradition. Matt Busby was a legend, and rightly so. Now, with reputations counting for everything, one man's loss became another's gain. And benefiting was Bobby Charlton, one of the few who could bring credibility in the eyes of the public. For Bobby it was a return from the wilderness. Following his Testimonial match against Glasgow Celtic and a tribute dinner, he left to join Preston North End as player/manager. Deepdale was not a happy hunting ground, and a subsequent foray as director at Wigan Athletic in 1983 (alongside Freddie Pye, Reuben Kaye and current Chelsea supremo Ken Bates) proved equally torrid. Bobby Charlton had severed all connections with Manchester United. When I was back as coach at the club he was just another ex-player who would occasionally call for match tickets. And, what few people may be aware of, he had also fallen out with Matt Busby. In fact, much as it hurt Matt, there was no communication between them for years. I witnessed the ill-feeling at first hand during a tribute dinner for Jimmy Murphy. Bobby was asked to speak, something he felt uncomfortable with in those days. On this occasion, though, he was more eloquent than usual. He gave a wonderful tribute to Jimmy, although the rest of us who were gathered were struck by the strident way he laid all the responsibility for his success at one man's door. With Matt Busby sitting at the top table, Bobby said that whatever he had achieved in football, there was one man, and one man only, to whom he owed his career. It was an incredible snub. Matt was next to speak. Like Bobby, the boss was ill at ease in such situations and he did his best to convey his thoughts to the room. In his own way he tried to explain the way things had been at Old Trafford, that Jimmy knocked the rough edges off, then he polished the diamonds. I can only imagine that he was deeply hurt by the inference that he had no influence on Bobby Charlton's career, that Jimmy was the sole figure who shaped his destiny.

I don't know what was the root cause of the Busby/Charlton row, but whatever the reason, I took no pleasure in it. Bobby and Matt did eventually make up, but the mere fact that they'd fallen out in the first place was another example of the gradual eroding of the Old Trafford spirit. I was saddened to witness it, but not totally surprised. I remembered a previous conversation during a visit from Bobby's brother Gordon. He called to see me in Swansea and we got around to discussing Bobby and Jack's futures. I thought Jack would be okay, but feared for Bob. Gordon said: 'There's more steel about Bob than you realise.'

If it comes as a surprise to know that the boss and Bobby didn't see eye to eye for several years, it was nothing compared to the shock I felt at seeing the tattered remnants that remained of the friendship between Matt Busby and Jimmy Murphy. From the moment they'd joined the club after the War they were the perfect foil for one another: Matt, the man of few words, the quiet authoritarian; Jimmy, the wonderfully warm Welshman who shouted at you, played with you, laughed with you and drank with you. Together they accomplished so much. Together they built a club.

The Munich air crash also revealed a friendship that transcended a mere successful working relationship. I stood with Jimmy and Bill Foulkes in a Munich hospital beside Matt Busby's bed, the boss in an oxygen tent and near death's door. I listened as Jimmy, in his husky Welsh tones, talked to his friend. This was the same man whom I found on the staircase of the

Stathus Hotel, sitting alone in the darkness sobbing his heart out. There was a bond between men, a bond I could never see broken.

After the crash Jimmy took temporary control of United in Matt's absence, guiding the club to that FA Cup final defeat by Bolton Wanderers. He had been promoted to assistant manager in 1955 and retained that position until '71. He also turned down several lucrative offers to take control of other clubs because Manchester United was his heart and soul. Everyone needs money to put food on the table, but Jimmy Murphy's life was not about pounds and pence. Football meant everything to him – in fact, he was anti anything which got in the way. He would speak to the press, but if their timing was wrong, if it interfered in him talking to his players, then that particular reporter could expect to be sent away with his ears ringing. It would be fair to say that Jimmy was anti-establishment and if Matt hadn't resumed control after Munich I reckon World War III would have broken out. If he'd had his way the only people allowed into the boardroom would have been the players. Jimmy was 63 when he finally stood down as assistant manager. His connections with the club were not cut completely, but he soon found himself marginalised in a way that lacked understanding of what he had achieved and what he still had to offer. As a coach I used to sit in the chief scout's office (Jimmy's old office) and wonder why Jimmy wasn't there.

It was agreed during Wilf McGuinness' spell as manager, and later implemented during Frank O'Farrell's reign, that Jimmy would accept a job as scout at United. He also received a nominal one-off payment. But the severance deal didn't stop there. Jimmy never learned to drive and travelled everywhere by taxi. The club informed him that they could no longer pay for his taxis and they also stopped paying his telephone bills. The financial aspect of this would no doubt lead to hardship further down the line, but it would have been the principle which rankled most with Jimmy. I've seen it written several times that he blamed Matt Busby for not doing more to help. The bitterness which was to sour their friendship festered away as Jimmy watched how others were treated. He travelled by British Rail, and yet others at the club were given their own car. To direct his discontent at Matt Busby, though, was not altogether fair.

I have never set out to defend the boss, but I have to be even-handed. Jimmy Murphy should never have been edged out of playing affairs at Old Trafford, but surely the responsibility for ensuring a man with so much still to offer remained was down to the man in charge of playing matters. He more than anyone else should have realised Jimmy's worth. I know that Matt Busby felt he was in an impossible position, in fact he told me as much. I was back as coach and things at the club were not going well. I was in the ticket office one morning and Matt walked in. I felt like a kid caught with my hand in the cookie jar because as a player you were never allowed in there. I almost forgot I was now a coach. The boss shook my hand and asked how I was doing. I said great and he put his arm around my shoulder and told me the manager needed help. He added: 'You put *your* arm around his shoulder, son.' Sometime later we met again. Things weren't as they should be at Old Trafford and I suggested the boss do something. I told him if he didn't the club wouldn't last nine months. He said: 'I can't son, I can't. If I try to help, I'll be accused of interfering. If I don't, I'll be accused of doing nothing.' And let's be honest here, what could he have done? He may have been perceived as this all-powerful figure at Old Trafford, but he hadn't even been able to get the board to honour their agreement to make his son a director. He'd even had his club car taken away because, as a director, he was no longer viewed as an employee. Jimmy and his family felt Matt should have fought his corner but I don't really think he had any other choice than to give the new regime its head.

Bobby Charlton may have eventually healed his rift with the boss, but by the time the wee Welshman passed away in 1989, he and Matt were strangers. I still cannot quite get my head around their falling out, how two men who between them built an institution could be allowed to drift so far apart. Manchester United has provided me with so many wonderful memories down the years, but witnessing the break-up of the Busby/Murphy partnership, the friendship, only brings sadness.

It should never be underestimated just what Jimmy Murphy contributed to the history of United. Bobby may have been scoring points when he stood up that day and said he owed his career to only one man, but it was certainly Jimmy who changed him from a good player to a great one. Former colleagues of mine accuse me of being two-faced when it comes to Bobby. I'm not. I'll be the first to admit that he was heralded as something special when he didn't deserve it, but I am also big enough to hold my hands up and give credit when it's due. As a young player at the club Bobby was blessed with fantastic skill, balance, the most incredible change of pace and a rocket shot. The brain and feet, however, did not work as one. I remember getting injured against Spurs in 1961 and playing the remainder of the game at centre-forward. I was marked by Maurice Norman, a giant of a centre-half, and I decided to move out to the left wing and at least draw one of the defenders. I pulled wide, but no-one came with me. Now, I was no longer a decoy, even in my strapped-up state I was a threat on goal. Bobby picked up the ball and I yelled for a pass. I kept shouting, but Bobby tried to take everyone on himself and ran up a blind alley. I went over to him as he lay on the ground and said: 'You brainless f——g idiot, thank God I don't have to play up here with you every week.' That was Bobby Charlton at *that* time. And there were players who didn't want him in the team. Not because they didn't like him as a lad, but because they thought he was difficult to play with. To this day some believe he wasn't a player. The fans and media, on the other hand, loved him. He was the most aesthetically pleasing footballer you ever saw, that balance and control, the blond hair, the searing shots from distance. In fact, I think people preferred one of Bobby's blockbusters that flew 20 yards wide to a Denis Law or Dennis Viollet tap-in from a few yards. It was just one of those things. Bobby looked good even when he wasn't. Enter Jimmy Murphy. He loved Bobby and spent a lot of time with him. He bollocked him for 'glory balls', for attempting the difficult when something simpler was more effective. He got Bobby thinking about his game. I can see Jimmy even now, laying into Bobby on a Tuesday morning. 'Bob, on Saturday you hit more glory balls in one game than I've seen in ten years. You looked great with those 40 and 50 yard balls. The crowd loved it . . . but so did their right-back.' In the early days I believe Bobby Charlton merited about a quarter of the plaudits he received, in the last five years of his United career he deserved everything that came his way. The brain and feet were then in perfect harmony. He'd become, with Jimmy's help, a great player.

In the same way that Jimmy Murphy felt Matt could have, and should have, done more to help him, so too Bobby has his critics. Some of those involved in the Munich crash are adamant he has been in a position to help since joining the board and has sat on his hands. I've heard this nonsense that Bobby was a changed man after Munich, but that's rubbish. Before the crash he liked a beer with the lads. He was never the life and soul of the party, but he wasn't aloof. He was the worst poker player I've ever seen in my life, but that didn't stop him joining in with the rest of us. Poor Bob was beaten before he'd even thrown down a card. He'd tell everyone that he only had a certain amount of money on him and after that he was stopping. And yet each time he'd be writing cheques. And if we talked about the match, Bobby would pick up his pint and say: 'I'm off if you're going to talk about football.'

There have been occasions when the Munich survivors have met and the consensus has been to make a decision without consulting Bobby. That is something I can never be party to. He is one of us and in the end deserves the chance to make his own mind up about what is the right thing to do. Sometimes, though, what he says and what he does are entirely different. When we were invited to the Champions League final in Munich (1998) each of us were asked by the media to talk. When my turn came I told the assembled press that I tried not to think about it every day (for the sake of my sanity) and that more often than not other people brought up the subject. Bobby spoke after me. He said: 'I'm not like Harry,' and that every morning in life he thought about the crash and the lads who died there. Well, if that's the case, he's had more opportunity than most to do something to help.

Louis Edwards' treatment of Matt Busby over Sandy joining the board; Bobby Charlton falling out with the boss; saddest of all, the breakdown of relations between Jimmy Murphy and Matt; the *World In Action* exposé; these are events which went against the grain. Louis and Martin have, over the years, become a target for United fans. They have watched as Martin Edwards has tried to sell the club on more than one occasion, they have watched a reticence to doff his cap at the past. All clubs need to move with the times, I've no complaints with that, but to suggest that the Busby Babes are not relevant to the modern United is an insult. The past casts its shadow over the present, but that doesn't have to be seen as negative. In recent years Martin Edwards and the club have acted, most notably when the survivors and the PFA's Gordon Taylor came up with the concept of the Munich Memorial Match. The return of Eric Cantona to Old Trafford for the game went against our wishes, but what could we do? To many it looked like Martin Edwards had used the match, an occasion that was about the 42 men who comprised Manchester United in 1958, to make up with Cantona. I suppose the ends justify the means and at least some of the people that matter benefited. Somehow it seems to have been forgotten that Louis Edwards' involvement in Manchester United, and certainly his rise to the position of chairman, is largely down to Matt Busby. And without his father's elevation to power there would have been no place at the top table for Martin. Forgotten too, is the closeness that once existed between the Edwards and Busby families.

The crash is not the overriding reason why so many Manchester United fans follow the club. The Busby Babes are. They were a group of young men who played the game with the freshness of youth. Today, Alex Ferguson has again bottled that essence of youth. The Old Trafford faithful enjoy the sweet smell of success, but they also recognise the way in which it's achieved. That is the legacy of the past, of Matt Busby, Jimmy Murphy, and all those who went to Belgrade. That is part of our heritage. That is something I suspect Martin Edwards doesn't want to understand.

XIII

MONEY TALKS

I was in the medical room at Old Trafford one Friday afternoon with Dave Sexton, the Scouse comedian George Roper, United's physio Laurie Brown and Joe Jordan. Although you weren't allowed to smoke, for obvious reasons, Dave was puffing away on his cigar. So I decided if the rules didn't apply to him, they didn't apply to me, and I lit up a cigarette. Joe, who'd been having a rub down after training, eventually left and the rest of us continued shooting the breeze. Eventually I doused my cigarette butt under the tap, pressed the pedal which lifted the heavy lid of the waste disposal bin and chucked it away. Suddenly there was an explosion and I was catapulted across the room. Laurie threw towels on the fire and I was left nursing burns and blisters all over my face and hands. The following Monday we were laughing and joking in the staff room and Dave Sexton said: 'Tell them what happened downstairs? "H" nearly gave his life for the club!' I know it was a throwaway line, but it hurt deeply. I snapped back: 'Aye, you're f——g right, and more than once too!'

My reaction to Dave's insensitivity probably says more about me than it does about him. I knew he didn't really mean anything by it, but it cut me like a knife. Some things I find hard to joke about. You see, I genuinely think of Manchester United as *my* club. It has been, and still is, a massive part of my life. It's so much a part of who I am. I care about what the club stands for, what Matt Busby created through his spirit and vision. It's why I can't help getting involved. For me, there's no switch that can be flicked to 'off'. It's once a United man, always a United man. And there have been occasions, long after I hung up my boots, when I've been drawn back in like a moth to a flame.

In the early '80s Robert Maxwell became an active player in British football. He ended up being reviled by fans from Oxford United and Reading for his abortive attempt to merge the two clubs to form Thames Valley Royals. He also turned his attentions on Old Trafford and came within a hair's breadth of gaining control of United.

I was at Rotherham United. They'd been second from bottom of the league and Emlyn Hughes had asked me to come along and help out. Looking back, I'd like to think I made a difference as the Yorkshiremen ended the season just missing out on promotion. During my time there the club was owned by Anton Johnson. I got to know him quite well. We weren't bosom buddies, but friendly in as far as chairman–employee relationships go. Out of the blue, Anton Johnson invited me to meet him in Southend (he also owned Southend United and Peterborough United). As it happened I was due to appear on a *This Is Your Life* show for Pat Jennings, so after the recording I caught the train south. Andrew McCutcheon, Johnson's financial advisor, picked me up at the station and drove me to the football club. I was treated like royalty before finally meeting Mr Johnson. He informed me of his plans to put together a regime at the club that included Sir Alf Ramsey and Bobby Moore (who I'd chatted to at the reception area where he was working). I was, according to him, 'the last piece in the jigsaw'. He was paying me a lot of compliments, in fact he was laying it on pretty thick. He said: 'You know I have a Roly-Poly,' adding that if his name was Harry Gregg he wouldn't need a Rolls-Royce to open doors. I was thinking this was some build-up and wondering what was next. Then, with no prior warning, he hit me with: 'What would it take to buy Manchester United?' I'll have to admit it caught me by surprise, but I said: 'You can't buy an institution.' Johnson said the person who was interested had been involved in another venture a few months earlier. Obstacles were placed in his way but it was something he wanted, so he went out and spent £80m. I said: 'You haven't told me who *he* is', and Johnson replied: 'Robert Maxwell.'

Like many ex-players I was finding work hard to come by at that time.

The mention of Maxwell and Manchester United was the chink of light I'd been looking for and I have to admit self-interest took over. I thought to myself that a takeover might provide a way back to my beloved Old Trafford. Foolishly, I gave Anton Johnson advice that would have been best kept to myself. I described the breakdown between Martin Edwards and Matt, that the Busby name was worth millions, and that if he could be recruited you would be on to a real winner. I also gave him background information on the United board – Martin Edwards, Denzil Haroun (Martin's uncle), Alan Gibson and Billy Young. Johnson thanked me and said he would be in touch. It was the last I heard from him.

No-one likes to be used, but that's exactly what Anton Johnson and Robert Maxwell did to me. They clearly had no intentions of taking me on board, or anywhere else for that matter, they just wanted information and I'd duly obliged. In the end my pursuit of work took me to the Middle East. I was in Kuwait when Derek Potter from the *Daily Express* phoned. Derek was a good friend, a thoroughly decent bloke who demonstrated the sort of integrity I admire in a journalist. I'd taken the call in the hotel foyer and after a brief chat about families and the like I dangled the carrot: 'Do you want a good story?' I'd had plenty of time to think. I now knew I'd let my desire to get back to Old Trafford cloud my judgement. There was no way Robert Maxwell was the sort of man you'd want running a club like Manchester United. To him it would just be another commodity. There were a few ex-pats around in the hotel lobby so I gave Derek my room number and said to phone me back in five minutes. I asked him was he sitting down, then told him everything I knew about Maxwell's attempt to buy Manchester United. This revelation was greeted by stunned silence. Four hours later he called me back to say that himself and Mike Dempsey (the newspaper's northern sports editor and a United fanatic who'd once applied for Walter Crickmer's job as Secretary) were booked on a flight to London. They'd phoned Robert Maxwell and he hadn't denied the story. Negotiations between Robert Maxwell and Martin Edwards broke down in February 1984, but the death knell for the deal was undoubtedly the *Daily Express's* exposé on the whole affair. A year later and I was working as coach at Carlisle United. Derek Potter phoned me up and said: 'I just wanted to thank you, "H", I've just won my first international cap.' It turned out that Derek had been awarded Sports Journalist of the Year for the Maxwell story.

I often wonder how strange it was that I came to have such a prominent role in Maxwell's demise. More bizarre, though, was my part in the Michael Knighton takeover bid almost a decade later. By then I was completely out of the loop, back living in Ireland and running a hotel, The Windsor, in Portstewart. I hadn't even seen the television footage of Michael Knighton's surprise entrance on the opening day of the season when, decked out in a United kit, he juggled the ball and fired shots into the net at Old Trafford. It wasn't long, though, before I, like every other United ex-player or fan, was following the Knighton saga closely. Before too long I was thinking to myself: 'What has my club come to?'

By sheer coincidence, I met Michael Knighton not long after his ball-juggling antics. I was invited across to the Cresta Hotel in Altrincham for a Nat Lofthouse charity dinner. It was formal dress and I was wearing a white tuxedo. There was only one other person in the place with the same colour of tuxedo as me. I was introduced to Michael Knighton and said: 'I'm glad to see you're wearing a white tuxedo. At least there's two wine waiters here.' He laughed and said how nice it was to meet me. He seemed perfectly charming.

The following day I paid a visit to Old Trafford and ran across Matt Busby, who had been sitting at the top table with me during the Nat Lofthouse dinner. He was in the grill bar with Les Kershaw, chief scout at the club. Les was looking after Matt for the day and they asked would I join them. Les has a university degree and I laughed and joked with the boss that it was just as well that we didn't need qualifications like that in our day. Eventually Matt and Les left and it immediately struck me as odd when Matt's best mate Paddy McGrath came over. Paddy was also a good friend of mine and a United supporter from the year dot. However, I couldn't figure out why he hadn't made his presence known to the boss. After the usual chit-chat Paddy asked me if I had a contact number for Amir Madani. I told him I didn't and asked why he wanted it. His words were: 'I know someone who can break the Knighton deal', something, I might add, which appeared to be signed, sealed and ready for delivery. I headed to my daughter's house in Ashton Lane and immediately phoned a friend of mine, Bob Russell, at the *Daily Mirror*. Bob could not provide me with the number Paddy was chasing but, by way of consolation, he did offer a contact for United director, Nigel Burrows.

I called Burrows and said: 'You might not know me. I'm six foot odd, I used to keep goal . . .' Before I could continue he blurted out: 'Harry Gregg! When I stood at the Stretford End, you taught me how to swear.' He continued with this patronising patter for a while and then I told him that I might know of someone who could break the Knighton deal. Burrows interrupted. He was adamant that the deal could not be broken, and that he and Amir would have bought the club themselves had they known Martin Edwards was selling his shares. Burrows added that the first he knew of it was when Maurice Watkins told him Edwards was planning to buy property in the Lake District. He thought Martin had financial problems and couldn't figure out where he was getting the cash. He'd then confronted him, but the deal with Knighton was already done. Before putting the phone down I explained to Burrows that he would not hear from me again unless I could turn up incontrovertible evidence that the deal between Knighton and Edwards could indeed be broken. He was very sceptical.

After our little chat, I phoned Paddy McGrath and asked for the name of the person who could break the deal. He started by saying there were two, including one in Manchester. I stopped him before he could go any further. Manchester was like a village, it would be playing too close to home. The other, he said, I knew very well. His name was Roy Dixon. A former shareholder at United and solicitor by trade, he had moved into property development and was now living in the Isle of Man. I'd first met Roy when he'd shown Carolyn and I around his house. He was moving to a newly built property and we were looking to buy our first home together. It was a guided tour I'll never forget because I ended up pushing on these beautiful mahogany doors thinking it was a wardrobe, only to find it was the doorway to an ensuite bathroom.

Paddy gave me Roy's number in the Isle of Man and I called him up. As with my introduction to Nigel Burrows, I said: 'Do you remember a guy, six foot two with blue eyes, who went through a wardrobe which he didn't realise was an ensuite?' 'Bloody hell, Harry Gregg!' I told him I was led to believe he could break the Knighton deal. He confirmed that he had that power and I enquired as to whether it could be achieved within the letter of the law. He said it could be done legally because there'd be so much shit hitting the fan that there would be no need for anything else. I asked what part he wanted in it. He told me none. And his parting words to me were: 'You're as big a bloody fool, Harry Gregg, as ever you were. Borrow £10m, buy the club, let it sit, and then go public.' Not bad advice in hindsight; Manchester United PLC is worth considerably more than £10m today. I hadn't thought about it before but, far fetched as it might sound, I decided to see what I could do. Straight away I tried to call Andy McCutcheon, the same financial advisor who'd met me at Southend for Anton Johnson. I left messages on his answer machine that I needed £10m to buy United. I scrabbled around looking to borrow the money, calling absolutely anybody who I thought might be able to help. Buzzing around my head was the thought that my name, and with Matt Busby supporting, would give me a decided edge against Martin Edwards, or anyone else for that matter. In the end, though, it was one brick wall after another. There was no way I could stump up the money, so I contacted Nigel Burrows again. I gave him Roy Dixon's telephone number and he thanked me very much for my help. I waited for further word from Nigel Burrows.

Days passed and Burrows was not returning my calls. Finally, I quite literally *tracked* him down. He was on a train on the Manchester line and by mobile phone he proceeded to tell me that he'd spoken to Roy Dixon, and of his grand plans for United. Martin Edwards would be out, he would take over as managing director. It would be a much more democratic board, with him at the helm, of course. And there was no way Bobby Charlton would be allowed to become chairman, because, in Burrows' words: 'He doesn't have the brains for business.' He added: 'God forbid, but when Matt dies, Bobby will become president.' My initial thought was: 'This guy's playing God.'

Maybe it was his attitude during that phone call, or a gut feeling that he was far from being a knight in shining armour, but I started having second thoughts about what was happening. I mulled over in my head the past couple of decades at United – the Maxwell bid for power and Martin Edwards' desire to sell; Knighton's arrival on the scene; and men like Burrows whom I'd helped without really considering if he deserved it. And I don't mind holding my hand up and admitting that at that moment I decided to change horses in mid-stream. I had been staunchly anti-Knighton, but was now of the opinion that he couldn't possibly be any worse than the guys already in control at Old Trafford. I mean, what had they really achieved in the time since I'd left the club? They'd employed some managers who were an embarrassment and failed miserably to build on the foundations laid by Matt Busby. I decided to phone Michael Knighton.

Knighton listened as I confessed to being the one who had given away the means to stop his deal. He broke down. Adamant that there were no skeletons in his closet, he confessed that the man who was trying to crucify him was Robert Maxwell. Knighton believed that Maxwell was jealous because of his own failed attempt to buy United. Maxwell's newspapers had been trying to dig up any dirt they could find, anything that would scupper his chances of completing the deal. I told Knighton to stick with it, that I was now in his camp. We chatted again after that and he would enlighten me as to the goings-on in board meetings. I, in turn, gave him enough to keep many of the people at Manchester United in check. It wasn't a particularly smart move on my part. Michael Knighton used some of this background info at a board meeting and the next day he rang to say that I would probably be getting a call. He'd told the board he'd been invited to a meeting with someone at the Piccadilly Hotel and they'd given him an insight into the men sitting around the table. Nigel Burrows was immediately convinced he'd been talking to Harry Gregg. Michael denied knowing me and when, sure enough, the call from Burrows came, I did likewise. I asked what it was he wanted from me. The answer . . . the standing of his fellow board members in the city. I rang Knighton again and he furnished me with the information I needed. Nigel Burrows was not quite so cocky when I eventually called back. Only a couple of directors got a clean bill of health, and Burrows wasn't one of them. His muck-raking had just backfired and our conversation ended abruptly. Here was a guy with grand plans for United, and yet, as was to come to light further down the line, he hadn't the money to pay for the shares which he bought from Alan Gibson. In fact, he finished up doing a Lord Lucan and disappearing overseas.

The path looked clear for Knighton. If he could raise the £10m asking price the club was his. It looked to be plain sailing and I was taken completely by surprise when I heard the news that he was withdrawing from the deal. I couldn't believe he was going to pack it in now after all he'd been through. I tried desperately to speak to him, finally giving up at 11 o'clock that night. I was desperate to tell him not to throw in the towel.

Michael Knighton told me he'd pulled out of the deal because Martin Edwards, with whom, incidentally, he got on well, had phoned at midnight to say that if he took over the rest of the board would resign. To me, that would have just been an added bonus, and I told Michael so. I think, though, that by this stage he'd just about had enough. Men like Michael Knighton never stay down for long, though, and a year later he was back in the game.

Michael was offered the chance to buy Peterborough United and he phoned me in Ireland to find out if I could make a few enquiries about the club and what sort of money might be involved. I rang Maurice Evans, who was at Oxford United. I'd given Maurice his first coaching job (at Shrewsbury) and thought he might be able to help because the owner of Peterborough had previously been on the Oxford board. I gathered what information I could and called Michael back. I told him he'd be daft to buy Peterborough because by comparison with Carlisle United it had little to offer. From the day and hour Bob Stokoe took me to Carlisle as coach I'd been convinced this was a set-up with enormous potential. A former First Division club, there was no reason why, with the right backing, it couldn't be a major player again. Michael wasn't convinced, but fate was to intervene. Not for the first time Carlisle United found itself in the financial mire. Closure looked imminent, and who should they call for help, but me? The very fact that the club's financial director Robin Laddell phoned me in Ireland was proof of how desperate the situation was, for I'd left Cumbria under something of a cloud.

Following my stint as coach, and against my better judgement, I'd accepted the manager's post in succession to Stokoe. And if I wasn't aware of what lay in store, it became abundantly clear at the first board meeting I attended. Andrew Jenkins asked if anyone knew a millionaire. The club's vice-chairman, John Sheffield, shook his head, followed by everybody else around the table. Robin Laddell stood up and said how a League Cup run could help the club's precarious financial position, followed by a good FA Cup campaign. I sat there thinking that it was all going to be bloody well down to me and I'd only just got here. When I was given the opportunity to speak I told the board: 'Gentlemen, if you ran your business the way you run Carlisle Football Club, you would be broke.' I advised the board that the only way to survive was to put the club on a sound financial footing. The rest would then fall into place. My advice went unheeded and things eventually went from bad to worse. It came to a head when the club's secretary was sacked for financial impropriety and the bailiffs landed one morning. And who was the mug who came to the rescue? On that occasion I even wrote a personal cheque for £15,000 and had it delivered to the chairman's business. Sadly, my support for Carlisle United Football Club would eventually be thrown back in my face.

I had no reason to doubt that Carlisle United appreciated my contribution, particularly as, at my last board meeting, the chairman, Andrew Jenkins, had taken me aside to tell me no-one had done more for the club and that I would have a job there for life. I'd been something of a footballing nomad for a few years and that evening I went home and told my children that dad wouldn't be moving anymore. On the Tuesday evening I went down to the ground to watch the part-timers and schoolboys train. The chairman was there and he asked would I meet with our two new directors (Aiden Liddell and Arthur Church). They had not been at the last board meeting and Andrew wanted me to enlighten them as to my future plans. Forty-eight hours later I was out on my ear. I'd gone down to training as usual, passing former England international turned journalist Ivor Broadis on the way in. Andrew Jenkins met me and together with vice-chairman John Sheffield we went for a chat. Andrew seemed agitated and I asked what was the matter. He mumbled something about me having an overbearing personality and that the board thought it would be a good idea to let me go and then bring me back in three months. I couldn't believe what I was hearing. I stopped Andrew and reminded him that I'd only just forked out £75 of my own money to cover one of the players' maintenance payments and an electricity bill. The chairman said that would be taken care of and repeated the line about my overbearing personality. I walked over to the window and called Ivor Broadis. I said: 'These boys are telling me I've got the sack.' Ivor turned to him and said: 'Andrew, are you off your f——g head, the man has saved the club.' I told him to leave it be.

Given this background, and the on-going court case between Carlisle and myself over unpaid contract severance money, I was the last person you'd expect they'd ring. During yet another of the club's crisis times I'd actually put our house on the market and offered £250,000 through Andy McCutcheon to buy the club. But to give you an idea of how strained our relations had become Andrew Jenkins came out in the newspaper and said he would never sell to Harry Gregg (despite this Andrew and I remain good friends). Now, here was Robin Laddell pleading with me to rescue Carlisle United. As it was, his timing could not have been better. I couldn't help, but I knew a man who could.

I phoned Michael Knighton on his mobile. He was on the way down the M6 from his castle in Scotland. I begged him not to take the first turn-off, but to call by Carlisle United's ground and take a look for himself. I stressed, as I had done many times before, the geographical position, the fact that the nearest club to the south was Preston North End, to the north, Queen of the South. I added that all 19 and a half acres, training ground and car park, belonged solely to the club. I gave it the hard sell and left Michael to it. Initially he thought the ground looked a bit scruffy, but I could tell he was warming to the task. Eventually I got two parties together. Michael decided to buy, along with Barry Chato, ex-chairman at Bolton Wanderers. I was invited to join the board and throw in a few quid of my own, but I declined. To be honest, I didn't have the money as I'd ploughed my savings into The Windsor Hotel.

Michael subsequently helped settle my dispute over outstanding monies. I'd led Carlisle to believe I had the backing of the Managers and Secretaries Association, my ace card, but it wasn't true. In reality I hadn't the proverbial pot to piss in and half of the money I received in an out-of-court settlement went on legal bills.

I've no doubt there are Carlisle United fans who, given recent developments at the club, are cursing me for introducing Michael Knighton. And yes, Michael has hired and fired, committed the cardinal sin of dabbling in playing matters and made decisions I don't agree with. But, what should also be remembered is that had I not introduced Michael Knighton to Robin Laddell there is a very good chance Carlisle United would be out of football. Instead, the club was given a reprieve. Michael has now sold Carlisle and I hope that in hindsight the supporters can recognise his contribution. They have a superb new stadium and even if grant aid helped offset costs, it was a project that required a driving force. That driving force was Michael Knighton.

I've kept in touch with Michael and been over to the club a few times in recent years. Despite the flak that came his way, he was as flash as ever. To be honest, I can't help liking the man. He has no qualms about setting himself up to be shot at and you've got to admire that. What would have happened if he'd succeeded in buying Manchester United? Well, there are times when I dread to think. It very nearly happened, though, and whenever we meet Michael always says: 'Good God, Harry! The things you and I know about United.'

XIV

THE IMMORTALS

In the same way that beauty is in the eye of the beholder, so too is analysis of the *beautiful game*. Stop 100 football fans streaming out of any stadium and ask them to pick their favourite 11 players and it's a safe bet you'll get 100 different replies. I've witnessed at first hand many of the game's greatest players during my career, affording me a privileged position from which to chose my World XI. The following line-up is defined by a single parameter – at some point I've played with, against, or in the same tournament as these footballing virtuosos.

Although I must doff my cap to the likes of my countryman Pat Jennings, Russian legend Lev Yashin, Brazilian stopper Gilmar and Jack Kelsey, I can say without the slightest hesitation, that my goalkeeper is Germany's Bert Trautmann. An ex-paratrooper, he was captured in Belgium in early 1945 and eventually imprisoned in St Helens (Lancashire). Whilst playing in the prison team he attracted the attention of the local amateur side St Helens FC. Bert married one of the prison wardens' daughters, chose not to be repatriated, and was spotted by Manchester City. City had a big Jewish following and fans were so incensed at the club signing a German that they boycotted games and marched with banners protesting against Trautmann's inclusion.

I first watched Bert Trautmann a few months after crossing the Irish Sea to join Doncaster Rovers. I travelled the 18 miles by train to watch Manchester City play Sheffield Wednesday at Hillsborough and couldn't believe this guy in goal. Tall, blond, in fact the archetypal Aryan, he was in total command of his area. Everything Bert did was text book. Acutely aware of his position in relation to attacks, agile and incredibly courageous, he plucked crosses out of the air with an eye-catching artistry. Then there was his unique distribution. It was not an over-arm throw, more a whipping wrist-like action in which his elbow never left his side. Economy of effort, yet the ball was dispatched rapid fire and rarely off target. Everything about him impressed me. Years later when I moved to Manchester United he was the one and only goalkeeper I tipped my hat to. After local derbies I rushed out to buy the local papers, praying the hacks considered me as good as Bert. And I wasn't the only one who worshipped Bert Trautmann. The same City fans who had initially baulked at the idea of a German in their team were won over. On the Maine Road terraces they idolised their Teutonic top man. We became friends, and sadly I was there the day his career came to an end in ignominious fashion. United had no match and I went along to Maine Road to watch him play against West Ham United. The ball floated across the box and Bert missed it by the proverbial country mile – Geoff Hurst heading it into the empty net. Bert, possibly for the first time ever, lost his cool. Adamant that he had been pushed, he called to the referee. The official ignored Bert's pleas, turned his back and pointed to the centre circle. Completely out of character, Bert picked the ball out of the net and began running upfield. I knew what was coming next and sure enough he kicked the ball against the referee's backside. Before the gob-smacked official could put the whistle to his mouth, Bert pulled his jersey over his head and walked off. It was a sad end to a wonderful career.

My World XI centre-half is John Charles. I deliberated over whether to pick big John at defence or attack, such was his versatility. Most will think of him as a centre-forward, but he was also a magnificent defender. In the end I decided to play him at centre-half because such was his prodigious talent that he'd still score 20 goals from there. John Charles was a magnificent physical specimen. Built like a heavyweight boxer, you would never have imagined he could be so graceful. And yet, when the ball came to his feet he had the poise and grace of a ballet dancer. In the air there has never been, and never will be, anyone better. I remember when I was manager at Swansea and we were having a practice match. I was short a goalkeeper for the reserves and asked John if he would help out. He kept goals exactly like he played centre-forward, powering through the bodies with a masterful precision. I was so concerned for the confidence of my strike force that I actually went up to him at half-time and asked if he would mind letting a goal in.

They called him the 'Gentle Giant' and such was his strength that he didn't have to resort to foul play. When big John was shielding the ball it was like trying to negotiate your way around the back of a double-decker bus. John was an idol in Turin after a highly successful spell with Juventus and I witnessed at first hand his standing with the football-mad Italian public. I travelled to Italy with an old internationals team and this son of Swansea was mobbed on his arrival. There have been other great centre-halfs like Billy Wright and Jackie Blanchflower, but in more ways than one John Charles was a man apart.

Next up are my full-backs. Right-back is Nilton Santos, captain of Brazil's 1958 World Cup-winning team. Anything Cafu can do now, or has done for the past decade, Santos did before him. He could defend when required, but like any good Brazilian he could play. And don't let talk of the *beautiful game* fool you; like most of his compatriots he could take care of himself. In fact, in the 1954 World Cup quarter-final war with Hungary (which became known as the Battle of Berne) he received his marching orders after a punch-up with Josef Bozsik.

Left-back is Roger Byrne, and not, I must stress, through sentiment. I was very conscious when I sat down to pick this team that I would not let sentiment cloud my judgement. I have chosen Roger for one reason and one reason only, his ability on a football pitch. I have had the pleasure of playing behind some superb full-backs for my own country – Len Graham, Alfie McMichael, Dick Keith and Billy Cunningham – but none were better than Roger Byrne. He started his career as an outside-left and carried that technical ability into his defensive duties. He was quite a sight to behold when he robbed an opponent inside his own box, then threw two dummies with almost carefree abandon. He was also very, very quick. I know that to some observers Roger could appear aloof, almost arrogant, but that was just a result of the self-belief that characterised his game.

There was also another string to his bow. I was fortunate to play under two great captains, Danny Blanchflower and Roger Byrne. Your captain isn't always your best player, but Danny and Roger Byrne were both great players *and* great captains.

My right-half is Franz Beckenbauer; left-half is Duncan Edwards. Beckenbauer started out as a wing-half (or midfield as they call it today) and he was unbelievable. We played Bayern Munich in a friendly and he took the ball from his goalkeeper on the edge of the box. A few seconds later I was diving at his feet, the only touch I got to pick it up out of the back of my net. A majestic player, even in his younger years the *Kaiser* had a presence on the football pitch. Of course he eventually moved back to play sweeper. Now many, including Bobby Moore, have successfully moulded themselves into the *libero* role, but only one, Franz Beckenbauer, played it properly. When the ball is with the opposing winger and he is being closed down by the full-back, all sweepers drift in between full-back and centre-half to snuff out the danger. If the winger decided not to take on the full-back and instead crossed the ball, the centre-half is suddenly isolated one-on-one. Not with Beckenbauer. He held back, so if the winger swung the ball in, he could cover that eventuality as well. As intelligent footballers go, the *Kaiser* had few, if any, peers.

Duncan Edwards was a phenomenon. He didn't truly understand how good he was, or what he'd achieved in his young lifetime. I remember the lads dishing out some stick on the train coming back from the match with Arsenal (our last before heading to Belgrade). It was around the time that Billy Wright was coming to the end of his England career and they were slagging young Duncan, saying he was Billy's natural successor as captain. Duncan said: 'Na, na, Mark [Jones] is a better centre-half than me.' So self-effacing, he had absolutely no perception of his worth. Duncan was also a voracious trainer, he couldn't get enough of football. He would have played night and day. Despite his youth, Duncan was immensely strong. With those huge thighs and barrel-chest, he was a force of nature. I've seen it said that he feared no one, and although he was brave, that is not strictly true. I remember Northern Ireland's Jimmy Jones putting the fear of god into Duncan at Windsor Park during an international. Duncan Edwards was a great player; whether he would have become the greatest we will never know. Fate intervened, depriving us of the chance to see that unfulfilled potential realised.

Choosing Beckenbauer and Edwards was not as easy as it may appear. To select this prized pair, I had to disregard players like Danny Blanchflower, Wilbur Cush, Dave Mackay and Brazil's Didi. Likewise, when I considered my forwards, it required considerable soul-searching to finalise the line-up.

At inside-right I've gone for Peter Doherty. He was my mentor, but I can say hand on heart that my admiration for the man did not influence this decision. It was based on the opinions of his peers and on the year when I joined Doncaster Rovers and Peter was player–manager. Bill Shankly, Matt Busby, Stanley Matthews, Joe Mercer, Raich Carter – all regarded Peter as one of the greats. Carter, who would admit to being a conceited man, once spoke at a dinner in Old Trafford when I was there as coach. He talked about how he was the main man at Derby County when they signed this Irishman. After Peter's first game the newspapers were full of stories about this flame-haired Irishman. Raich wasn't best pleased that Peter had stolen his thunder, so the next match he tried that bit harder. Peter still stole the show. Carter upped the ante again, but Peter was still hogging the headlines. He admitted to doing this for a month to no avail and finally gave up trying to better Doherty's displays. Carter said he was a genius.

Even towards the end of his playing days he was incredible. At Doncaster we had a right-winger called Bert Tindell, a very good player. The idea was that Peter would start at inside-right and when he ran out of steam he and Bert would swap to give him a rest on the flank. It never happened. Peter was 41, but he could still run all day. In fact, he remains the only human being I have ever seen froth like a thoroughbred. Just like that fine coating of white that covers a horse after a race, Peter's shirt would be covered in this froth. I also witnessed him on many occasions betting a penny against a pound that he could lose a player at throw-ins. Peter would tuck his trousers into his socks and, still wearing his blazer, would do just that. No one ever got the better of him in training. There are two words you shouldn't use lightly – great and genius. Peter Doherty was both.

Inside-left could so easily have been John White, Johnny Haynes, or Jimmy Greaves – probably the most talented English-born finisher in my lifetime. All wonderful players. Or could it have been Hungarian Ferenc Puskas. He was the man who made the Mighty Magyars tick, who destroyed England at Wembley in 1953. 'The Galloping Major', as he was known, was an unlikely looking footballer. For most of his career he could best be described as portly, but he was deceptively quick. Puskas possessed a masterful football brain and a devastating shot in the left foot he always favoured. He left his native Hungary in 1956 and following a year in Austria, joined Real Madrid. I was lucky enough, or maybe that should be unlucky enough, to play against that wonderful Real side. Really and truly, that team, and in particular Puskas, was a sight to behold. He beat me with a back-heel and I remember castigating myself, saying: 'For God's sake Harry, at least make it look hard.' But to play against this man was awesome. He never appeared hurried, was never out of breath, and as a goalscorer he was unbelievable. His record at international level – 83 goals in 84 games – is second only to Pelé. And it is Edson Arantes do Nascimento, Pelé to you and me, who gets the inside-left berth. He emerged onto the world scene in 1958, a lithe black youngster from the Brazilian shanty town of Tres Coracoes. Blessed with agility, athleticism, amazing close control, he took football by storm. Searching for a weakness in his game is a futile exercise. A supreme goalscorer, Pelé had an unerring knack of reading the game in the most extreme situations, of remaining calm and in control when the battle raged all around. He could hang in the air like a Mockingbird, dispatch the fiercest of shots with either foot, and destroy a defence with one of those trademark explosive dribbles. And among the countless goals he scored for Santos and Brazil, none surpassed that strike as a 17-year-old in the World Cup against the host nation Sweden. With his back to goal he killed the ball on his chest, chipped it over his head, and volleyed into the bottom right-hand corner. What a player. What a man!

There are numerous candidates for the right-wing spot, including Tom Finney, and the *Wizard of Dribble* Stanley Matthews. The amazing thing about Matthews was that defenders knew exactly what he was going to do, but they still couldn't tackle him. He would stop you, then drop his shoulder and go the other way. But it is not Stanley Matthews whom I've chosen, but a player with a gift for the unexpected. Another Brazilian, it's Manoel Francisco dos Santos (Garrincha to you and me). Born into the slums of Pau Grande and crippled by polio at an early age, he learned to run on his disfigured right leg. Known to supporters as the *Little Bird*, Garrincha had a box of tricks that left defenders clutching at thin air. Carlos Alberto, that star of the World Cup in Mexico, gives an insight into Garrincha by saying that it was he, not Pelé, that the Brazilians looked for with a pass. I saw him in Sweden (1958) when I played, and also from the stand in 1966 when I attended many of the World Cup matches. He had the ability, even then, to excite, to make the hair on the back of your neck stand to attention with sheer skill.

On the other flank I can talk about another Real Madrid star, Gento; Italian international Ghiggia, who was once sent off at Windsor Park; or a very underrated *shuffling* winger, Eddie Gray of Leeds United. But it eventually boils down to a straight choice between two Irishmen. The first, Charlie Tully, was rightly crowned 'The Clown Prince of Paradise' during his time with Glasgow Celtic. Charlie was one of the funniest men I've ever met and one of the most talented. I saw him torment England's full-back, none other than Alf Ramsey. At one stage Charlie put his left foot on the ball, pulled up his sleeve and pretended to be looking at his watch. Then he egged Alf on to try and tackle him. Charlie also scored once direct from a corner kick. The referee disallowed it and ordered the kick retaken. So Charlie went back and did it again. He played his football like he lived his life – with a smile on his face. But the No 11 shirt goes to Belfast boy George Best.

I remember taking my Shrewsbury Town team along to The Hawthorns to watch West Bromwich Albion play Manchester United. I wanted the lads to see Bestie. In the first half he was diabolical, after the break he produced an exhibition the like of which I've never seen equalled. Long ball, short ball, taking players on, you name it, he did it. In his day George Best was the complete footballer.

Finally, we come to centre-forward, and here I'm most definitely spoilt for choice. There have been some wonderful centre-forwards, men like Tommy Taylor, who tragically died at Munich; Bobby Smith of Tottenham Hotspur; Tommy Lawton, who I saw play for Brentford at the end of his career. But my choice is another South American – Alfredo di Stefano. Born in Buenos Aires, di Stefano had everything. His work rate was phenomenal, a product of his athletic prowess as a young man in local road races. He covered every blade of grass on the pitch, and he was as tough as they come. In my day when you played against foreign opposition the shoulder charge was virtually unheard of. Prevalent in the British game, I had learned to take care of myself and there was no one I was worried about meeting in a 50/50. Catching one of the continentals like that early in a European tie was a plus point, but not di Stefano as I learned to my cost. I ran into him one night and I swear it was like hitting a tree. It was one of those occasions when you were hurting, but did your best not to let the other man know. I think it says all that, when asked which player he would most liked to have signed for Manchester United, Matt Busby replied: 'Alfredo di Stefano.'

That completes my World XI. As for a system of play . . . well, that's irrelevant. Great players don't play systems, they just play. Compiling this team has provided me with food for thought. It's made me realise just how lucky I have been. People have often asked am I bitter at missing out on cups and championships through injury during my playing career? But to have crossed paths with Trautmann, Santos, Byrne, Charles, Beckenbauer, Edwards, Puskas, Doherty, Garrincha, Best and Pelé, is worth more to me than a sack load of medals and silverware.

XV

BRAINS OR BRAWN?

It would be wrong to suggest British football is at a crossroads. The truth is that the path of *brawn* over *brains* was taken decades ago. We've paid the penalty, and how, with a game so lacking in imagination and originality that it's difficult to see a way back. I'm loath to use that well-worn phrase, *Things ain't what they used to be*, for it's guaranteed to conjure up images of doddering old farts reminiscing through rose-tinted glasses. But this is no fuzzy nostalgia; as far as I am concerned it's fact. And who's responsible for the parlous state of the game today? Well, I lay the blame squarely at the feet of the football authorities that mistakenly assumed that coaching was the answer to all ills. Don't get me wrong, there's nobody believes in coaching more than me. Sadly, they overlooked the fact that there is a world of difference between good and bad coaching.

Nurturing and moulding young players can help natural talent to blossom; poor direction and those god-given gifts will only whither and die. Look around you at the modern game and for every Ryan Giggs there are countless footballers that are nothing short of automatons. Every ounce of skill and freedom of spirit has been squeezed out, leaving a collection of off-the-peg footballers completely lacking in style and substance.

The deterioration of our game started as far back as the 1950s, its origins in the formation of the Football Association's coaching academy at Lilleshall. It was meant for the good of the game, but unwittingly signalled its death knell. Most of us were too involved in playing to attend Lilleshall in those early days and the majority who went along had, with no disrespect, failed to make an impression in the higher echelons of the game. I can still see the photograph of those first coaching graduates. None of them were great players, but they all went on to secure great jobs. The coaching structure was geared not so much to the gifted footballer, but to the man with a little bit more upstairs. The academically inclined revelled at Lilleshall to the detriment of the game as a whole. Today, coaching certificates are handed out, not to football people, but to men who learned the game from books or on a blackboard. They may look the part with a bag of balls slung over their shoulder and tanned legs, but what have they produced? Where are the great swathes of skilful homegrown players their coaching methods have helped to develop?

At Liverpool there is Steven Gerrard, an outstanding prospect, Michael Owen, and at Leeds United a product of Merseyside, Robbie Fowler; at Manchester United we can point to Beckham, Scholes, Brown, Butt, Giggs, Keane and the two Nevilles; at West Ham there's Joe Cole, Jermaine Defoe and Michael Carrick; Arsenal have Ashley Cole; and I also admire Damien Duff. But with the numbers playing the game can this select band of gifted young players be considered enough of a return for such a supposedly advanced coaching structure?

These days clubs cast an envious eye at foreign players, in fact, we can't get our cheque books out quick enough. They pass better, have a better touch and, wonder of wonders, actually run at people. These were attributes British players used to possess in abundance. We were the envy of the world once, now the masters are being educated by their pupils. In fact, we're now at a juncture where foreign players are actually holding the very fabric of the Premiership together, hiding our flaws. The foreign invasion has even extended to the coaching structure at Manchester United, with a Portuguese and a Brazilian now at Old Trafford. What does that tell you about our own coaches?

And it is with the influx of foreign players that the FA has effectively indicted itself. When, after the 1978 World Cup finals, the Argentine duo Ossie Ardiles and Ricky Villa were permitted to join Spurs it was almost an admission that we weren't good enough. Sure you can point to ball players like Frank Worthington, Stan Bowles and Tony Currie, but these men were mavericks, free spirits who flouted convention and actually entertained. By this stage the English League was already obsessed with the physical.

Fortunately there were still exceptions to the rule, men whose methods of bringing forth the best in players are deserving of respect. They were not academics, products of courses and certificates, but *football men*. I was fortunate as a player to be guided by, as opposed to brain-washed by, some wonderful tacticians and man managers. As a lad at my hometown team Coleraine I fell under the spell of the then manager, an ex-Scotland international called Arthur Milne. A former Hibernian star and member of the 'Blue Devils' (as the international side were known), he had the knack of imparting what he'd learned during his own career. Coaching is not all about chalk on a blackboard, but passing on knowledge. Around me were experienced players like Kevin Doherty, Terry McCavana, Mickey Canning, Harry McCormick, Jackie 'Hatchet' McIlreavy and Frank 'Bunty' Montgomery. Bunty didn't stand on ceremony. If my goal kicks were not up to scratch he would often blast the ball back and order me to do better. When I joined Doncaster Rovers there were men like Kit Lawlor and Paddy Gavin. Thanks to Paddy I was soon able to strike the ball with the best of them. Minutes, hours, days, months were spent practising at the airfield near Belle-Vue. If you missed the target on a windy day you had to run about four miles to catch up with the ball. If I'd mastered kicking, it took a quiet word from my international skipper Danny Blanchflower to hone that skill. My second appearance for my country was against the Combined Services at Windsor Park. I was determined to show the folk in Belfast what I'd learned and with a howling gale at my back I was hammering kicks right over the crossbar of my opposite number, Sunderland's Willie Fraser. At half-time Danny whispered to me: 'We're playing in green, son.' I asked what he meant. He said: 'The crowd love it, the opposition love it, but we're playing in green.' Another lesson learned. That is a craftsman passing on his knowledge to an apprentice – that is coaching at its best.

In my lifetime there have been some wonderful coaches, each with their own idiosyncrasies. Bill Shankly was one of the most earthy and lovable characters you are ever likely to meet. His game was based on complete and total passion. I remember being in his company on the way back from an Old Internationals exhibition match against Lincoln City. One of the Lincoln players had caught Bill with a bad tackle and he was ranting and raving about what he would do if he ever met him again. Bill was 47 at the time. Shankly's successor Bob Paisley had a contrasting style. A man of few words, he was not just charming, but also incredibly knowledgeable. When questioned after one of Bruce Grobbelaar's trademark charges upfield, Bob said: 'He just gets the same money.' Bruce approached me after joining Liverpool (I was coaching at Old Trafford) and asked could he come and work with me. I refused to work directly with him out of respect for Bob, although I did advise him on occasions. There's no way I would have gone behind his back. My reward came many years later when a friend rang me from London. Bruce was launching his book and my mate said: 'I heard someone taking your name in vain today.' Bruce had stated categorically that he would have returned to Zimbabwe had it not been for Harry Gregg. I have respect for men like Matt Busby, Peter Doherty, Bill Nicholson, Bill Shankly and Bob Paisley.

In the modern era there have been coaches and managers who carried on the tradition. I have the utmost admiration for the way Alex Ferguson has gone about his work, on and off the field. He turned Manchester United around when the club was heading for skid row. Arsène Wenger is another. I knew little of the Frenchman when he arrived from Japan's 'J' League, but he transformed George Graham's double-winning team from a side with the reputation for being boring to a double-winning side with flair. Tony Adams was basically what I call a hammer-throwing stopper, but by the time Wenger had finished with him he was a totally different animal. That goal he scored on the last day of the season (2001–02) when he galloped upfield, played a one–two and slammed the ball home, was one of the best of the league campaign. Wenger's countrymen Vieira, Petit and Anelka were also introduced to completely change the club's outlook.

And from my own country there is Martin O'Neill. I don't know him personally, but what he has achieved with often meagre resources is outstanding. At Leicester, and to a lesser extent at Celtic, he has cut his cloth accordingly. He has time and again managed to get the best from players, no doubt learning from his own club manager Brian Clough. Cloughie could manage players better than most, evidenced by the number who went to other clubs for big money but couldn't reproduce what they had achieved under Brian. Martin O'Neill was one of the few, and I mean few, who would give his opinion to Clough. Always self-opinionated, he has demonstrated the strength of will to do things *his* way. Martin O'Neill has been touted as a future manager at Manchester United, and if you were to ask me what I think, I'd tell you that many of his decisions to date have proved that he's big enough to handle any job.

If poor coaching is destroying our game, then so too is money. And by that I don't mean the amount being paid to players. I don't begrudge what the players earn today because I've seen what it used to be like. When I was at Doncaster it was an ageing team. In the first week of May you went upstairs to get your wages and inside was a letter. It either read: 'Dear so-and-so, thank you for your past services. The club is delighted in offering you a contract for next season at....' (or) 'Dear so-and-so, thank you for your past services. The club is notifying you of your free transfer.' I've watched married men, brave and good men, getting their envelope and walking across the huge car park at Belle-Vue because they were terrified to open it. It's still a short life but at least today players know that if they've been sensible their wife and kids are taken care of. The problem with the massive sums of money bandied around is that today it's better to have a good agent than be blessed with wonderful football ability. They can secure a fortune for players who, in many cases, are patently not worth it.

The real problem with money is where it comes from. Television companies are now dictating when you play; football is no longer setting its own agenda. In the modern game it's all about marketing and merchandising. Replica shirts are sold by the bucket load, but gradually off-field activities are overtaking what's happening on it. Television has also become the medium to disseminate knowledge. Many are influenced by what they hear on television, which is not necessarily a good thing. There's more football on the small screen than ever before, but with it comes the burden of listening to the inane drivel which emanates from the so-called analysts (or pundits). Many of them were very good footballers in their time, but they don't seem to give thought to what they've done, to pass on their knowledge. Most of the time their comments go in one ear and out the other, though occasionally I hear a pearl of wisdom. Ruud Gullit, a player I thoroughly enjoyed watching, was once on a panel and he interrupted the presenter during a discussion about the *beautiful game*. He said that sometimes you had to play the long ball to earn the right to play a short one. I thought to myself: 'Thank God!' Here was a man who in the space of a few seconds had grabbed my attention with a simple statement that makes so much sense. Johan Cruyff is another who interests me with his opinions. Maybe it's a Dutch thing, but people can often simplify matters, see situations clearly and succinctly without turning everything into a theatre show. Sometimes the rubbish they talk now makes me want to tear my hair out. I mean there's a whole new language grown up around the game. When pundits talk of 'body open' and 'body closed', or 'pulling the trigger', I have to ask myself if I'm watching *Emergency Ward 10* or a John Wayne film.

In my own country the Sports Minister Michael McGimpsey set up a Task Force to look into the game's problems. Before this August body came into being I spoke with him, expressing my concerns about the state of the Irish League. He told me he welcomed my call and would contact me again when he returned from his holidays. That's the last I heard from him. I expect someone advised him to stay away from Harry Gregg, probably saying I was a troublemaker. However, the least he could have done was to have the courtesy to phone. I'm not bitter at the Minister's failure to ask me to provide some input, but in the end his initial list of recruits to the Task Force included quite a few men who couldn't find their way to an Irish League ground, let alone advise you on what was best for the local game.

Amongst the areas in need of improvement identified by the Task Force are toilets, terracing and stands. Well, you can have male and female toilets by the dozen, with powder rooms in every one, but if the product on the pitch is not good enough the people will continue to stay away. When the television cameras pan around Irish League grounds and see empty terraces it's not just sectarianism or facilities that's the problem. Only recently during a house move I found an old newspaper cutting under the carpet. There was a report of a Linfield versus Glentoran match. Danny Blanchflower was a young player with the Glens at the time and the attendance was 32,000. A modern clash between the Blues and the Glens attracts less than half that figure. It's all about priorities. The game should still be about players and what they do on the pitch.

Football needs good administrators, but the problem arises when the administrators start getting involved in coaching. These days the stage manager appears to know more than the magician. We have far too many little men in big positions. Unfortunately, they're well dug in and it will take an almighty battle to force them out.

So where does British football stand now in the grand scheme of things? After the failure of England, Scotland, Wales and Northern Ireland to qualify for the World Cup in 1994, the four associations changed their managers. There was reason for hope. Nothing really changed, though. England managed to beat Holland handsomely in Euro '96 before going out at the semi-final stage. But that was a victory against a Dutch side riddled with internal problems. 1998 and it was exit stage left again, although this time it could all be blamed on Beckham. Okay, England may have beaten Germany 5–1 in Munich, but has that proved to be anything other than a false dawn?

The 2002 World Cup demonstrated once and for all that there is now a new world order. When I came back from the Middle East about 20 years ago I talked about how African nations were catching up fast. But it's not strictly true. The Africans and Asians have indeed been making great strides, but the truth of the matter is that we have also been going backwards. I enjoyed the World Cup in South Korea and Japan, but not for the quality on show. There was drama, certainly, but the most pleasing thing was to see teams like Gus Hiddink's South Korea or the Senegalese play with a freshness and vitality. They actually looked like they were enjoying the game and surely that's what it's all about. Diego Maradona was lambasted in the press for comments he made about the tournament.

He thought that David Beckham made little impression as a player; that it was an average Brazilian team that won the cup, and a very poor German side which reached the final; and that Ronaldo didn't particularly deserve the tag of Best Player in the Tournament. Well, I have to agree with him on most counts.

As for the future of the game on these islands, well, I'd like to say we're on the way back, but I'd be lying. The game has deteriorated despite the massive interest at present, and it will continue to do so until something is done about our overall attitude. Players are fitter and stronger than ever before, but good athletes don't necessarily make good footballers. The emphasis is still on *brawn* over *brains*. I'm tired of hearing people emphasising the need to play the simple ball. A good player will instinctively know when to play the simple pass, but if we destroy the ability to improvise we will be left with players who can do nothing else other than the simple. Surely football also has to excite and entertain. Manchester United during the Busby Babes era had 'A' and 'B' teams which were run by a former insurance clerk and a former shoemaker. They were men who lived for the game, but didn't get bogged down in coaching and tactics. They watched young players and then went to Bert Whalley and said: 'There's this young lad and he's great.' They didn't get into details about how good his left foot was, or how he positioned himself, it was just that he caught their eye. The good players were eventually signed up, then passed on to Bert. He imparted his knowledge, polishing a few more rough edges, before handing them over to Jimmy Murphy and Matt. The point is that in the early days they were allowed to play. Nowadays natural ability is coached out of young players. If a child can do tricks with a ball at 11 or 12, yet by the time he's 15 or 16 he's too scared to try anything different, what does that tell us?

We have to realise that coaching is not about what it says in some manual. Football is about free expression, it's not something to be repeated like the Lord's Prayer. But then, what do we expect? It's like learning to drive from a manual written by someone who can't drive. They have also worked hard over the years to entrench this 'Sport For All' ethos. Now I am all for involving every section of society in sport, but the diluting of talent that has resulted is harming the game. I worked with Ian St John at a coaching course in Larne a few years back. During a break I said to him that the majority of the boys and girls would never make players if they lived to be a hundred. Their parents were paying good money for their child to take part, and I don't blame them for that. But in my day you played on the streets, the two best players picking from the kids lined against the wall. Those who couldn't play well sat and watched. Nowadays, everybody's getting picked, everybody's playing, it's only natural that standards are in decline. I could take it further and say that the coaches who can't coach should also be left on the wall.

For the past 40 years I've had one book on my bedside table. Written by an Austrian, Dr Willie Meisl, and published in 1955, it contains his thoughts on the game and its future. Willie was so far ahead of his time, so prophetic, that it's not far-fetched to call him the Nostradamus of football. If we are to pull back from the brink we could do worse than heed Mr Meisl's message that to systemise in youth is to blunt the mind. 'We must free our soccer youth from the shackles of playing to order along rails (in ruts as it were); we must give them ideas and encourage them to develop their own. Hard tackling we have always known, they need not study it. We must show them many of the world's best teams and stars and let them see whether they can pick their brains and imitate their movements. Later perhaps add some new twist to the thoughts and tricks thus acquired. Then they will produce something new, or at least original . . .' Originality . . . now there's a thought!

XVI

BACK TO THE FUTURE

When Nobby Stiles and his youth team walked into my Portstewart hotel in the summer of 1991 I could never have imagined the profound effect this group of youngsters would eventually have on Manchester United Football Club. The Neville brothers, Gary and Phil; London lad David Beckham; native Mancunian Nicky Butt; and a shy flame-haired boy by the name of Paul Scholes – to me they were just another group of young footballers with their sights set on winning the Northern Ireland Milk Cup. And win it they did. A week later at the Coleraine Showgrounds in front of 10,000 spectators the team's captain, David Beckham, raised skyward the Under-16 trophy. Over the next decade this baby-faced Essex boy would become the most famous footballer since George Best, and his teammates amongst the most successful players ever to wear the red shirt of United.

United's Milk Cup class of '91 was an exceptional collection of talent, with Keith Gillespie, Chris Casper and Ben Thornley also going on to make the first team at Old Trafford. And I recall eavesdropping as young Thornley called home from the pay phone in the hall of the hotel. 'Tell Dad we won! Tell him I scored and was man of the match!' God, it took me back. It was like watching myself all those years ago calling my mum in Ireland. I'm proud to say these lads stayed in my home and I'm proud to have followed their progress from boys to men, and to be able to say, hand on heart, that they've managed to remain largely unaffected. They retain an enthusiasm for the game which is refreshing to see. It's been written that the FA Youth Cup triumph in 1992 set these lads on the path to glory, helped them develop the winning habit, but I like to think the foundations for future success were laid the summer before on the Causeway Coast. It's something I'll never forget and it's pleasing to know others remember those early days too. Years later in Dublin Paddy Crerand attempted to introduce me to David Beckham's father, Ted. Before Paddy had finished, Ted interrupted to say: 'Sure, I know Harry. We met years ago at The Windsor.'

Beckham, Butt, Scholes and the Nevilles have been instrumental in the glory years of Alex Ferguson's Old Trafford reign. But one man provided the catalyst for this success. He is, in my opinion, the single most influential figure in Manchester United's history since Matt Busby . . . *l'enfant terrible* Eric Cantona. The Frenchman came along when United needed a hero, when the club needed someone, or something, to ignite what would eventually become a remarkable renaissance.

Let's be honest, Alex Ferguson's early years at Old Trafford were anything but successful. I think even Alex underestimated the size of the task when he replaced Ron Atkinson in November 1986, for this was a club that required drastic surgery, on and off the pitch. How much is United folklore and how much is based on fact I'm not altogether sure, but Mark Robins' headed winner against Nottingham Forest in the FA Cup quarter-final is credited with ensuring Alex Ferguson's survival. Success at Wembley, and against Barcelona in the Cup-Winners' Cup final, prolonged his stay, but the real turning point came on 26 November 1992 when Cantona arrived from Leeds United. A call from the Yorkshire club's chairman on an entirely different matter, followed by an off-the-cuff enquiry from Fergie, led to the bargain to end all bargains . . . Eric Cantona for £1.2 million! But it was not Cantona's signature which was the mark of Ferguson's genius, but the ability to recognise within a short space of time the role he could play at Old Trafford.

I once heard Alex Ferguson tell a story at a function in Belfast about Cantona's first day at United. Brian Kidd came to him after training and said the Frenchman wanted a bag of balls, he was staying to practise. Fergie admitted his first reaction was: 'Big-headed git, who's he trying to impress?' Suspicious of Cantona's motives he told Kidd to give him the balls, saying it wouldn't last. But it did. Not only that, but gradually the other pros and the youngsters started staying behind too. Despite his gut feeling that there was an ulterior motive, Alex Ferguson was shrewd enough not to intervene. He could have viewed Cantona's actions as usurping his authority, but had the foresight to let the situation develop. He recognised that Eric Cantona's influence was good for the players and the club. And how right he was.

On the field Cantona had everything. He possessed sublime skill and that priceless commodity . . . presence! With his genius came the little eccentricities, but they were a small price to pay for a man who ensured the first League Championship for 26 years. A perfectionist in every sense of the word, United's kit man at the time, Norman Davis, told me Cantona would spend a quarter of an hour in front of the mirror before going out on to the pitch – everything had to be just right. Bobby Charlton confirmed his popularity in the dressing-room, adding that the Paris-born player also had a wicked sense of humour. Bobby recounted how he tried to communicate with United's French recruit, receiving monosyllabic replies. Then one day Bobby asked Eric about his kids. He replied: 'Yes, my boys are going to a comprehensive.' Bobby felt a right prat when he realised he could speak English all along.

Cantona did give Alex Ferguson his fair share of headaches along the way, none more so than in 1995 when he launched that infamous kung-fu assault on a fan at Selhurst Park. I remember watching the incident on television; Cantona's sending-off; and then the fans verbally abusing him as he walked along the touchline. Then this guy runs about 20 yards to hurl insults and Eric snaps. I kept thinking to myself, what was different about this guy, they were all shouting things at him? Just what was it that this lad said to provoke such a reaction? I thought to myself, bloody hell it must have been bad. And as is my way, I mouthed at the screen: 'Go on, Eric, hit him again.'

I suppose I can relate to this incident more than most. After a match at Luton Town I became involved in an altercation with a supporter that landed me in serious trouble. Some fans rushed onto the pitch after the final whistle and one, a tall guy with a string tie, started saying what he was going to do to me. I had just swapped my cap and gloves to my left hand in preparation for shaking hands with the opposition and as he approached I pushed him out of the way and told him not to be daft. As I shook hands with Billy Bingham he came at me again, so I thumped him. He hit the ground and started to twitch, which really worried me. The police came on and Maurice Setters guided me away. In the dressing-room afterwards the Luton manager Sid Owen came in and apologised for the behaviour of the fans. We travelled from Luton to Euston Station where the press were waiting. And at Piccadilly Station in Manchester the snappers were out in force again. As I walked along the platform they backed away, taking pictures as they went. I let them get their shots and then said that was enough. One photographer (Munich survivor Peter Howard) was still crouched down, snapping away. I warned him two or three times that enough was enough. Finally, I threatened to put him under the train if he didn't get out of the way. Not the smartest remark under the circumstances and the next day there was a headline: 'Heavyweight Irish goalkeeper assaults fan and threatens to push fellow survivor under train.' Matt gave me a real roasting, refusing to listen to any justification for my actions. That said, when the Bedford Constabulary arrived at my house with a summons for my arrest, Matt and the club supported me 100 per cent. Matt told them that if they'd been doing their job the incident with the fan wouldn't have happened in the first place. Billy Bingham always tells the story of how Harry Gregg hit a fan who was only looking for his autograph. Well, I've never refused an autograph in my life.

I was in Alex Ferguson's company towards the end of Cantona's time at United. I made the comment that the last thing he would want to do was drop him. Alex turned to me and said: 'Hey, big man, you're right.' I'm positive Alex was relieved when Eric decided to call it a day. I don't think he ever wanted to be in the position where he had to go and say to the lad that he was dropping him. Disagreements over money were cited as the reason for Cantona's departure, but I feel he too could sense a diminishing of his considerable talents. If you look at Cantona's physique towards the end of his time at Old Trafford, his torso no longer had the same definition. Why else would he not have pulled on his boots again for another club?

And it was a decision I applaud. How often have we watched players carry on beyond their allotted time like ageing boxers who can't resist just one more fight? Eric Cantona got out when he was at the top. Footballers are their own harshest critics. I know that when I retired it was because I was beginning to question myself. I felt that I was not as brave, physically and mentally, as I had been earlier in my career. I desperately wanted to play on, but I'd set myself standards and wasn't prepared to fall below them. I am also of the firm belief that Manchester United was Cantona's spiritual home, the only place where he felt truly happy. Look at his record at other clubs, particularly in his native France. Alex Ferguson was the only manager who truly understood his occasionally flawed genius, probably the only manager who truly understood him as a man. In the end Eric Cantona was good for United and United was good for Eric Cantona.

Cantona influenced those around him as a player, but also in his attitude to the game. He was a master craftsman and instilled a belief, a confidence in the young players Alex Ferguson blooded during the early '90s. Ryan Giggs made the breakthrough as a 17-year-old in the spring of 1991. Then in the following few years those same youngsters who'd laughed and joked in the Windsor Hotel began to make their mark. Nicky Butt was the first to be handed his debut, a player in the Nobby Stiles mould. And when I compare him to Norbert, it has nothing whatsoever to do with that blinkered perception people have of him as a hard man. Nicky Butt, like Nobby, is an extremely intelligent footballer who, until the last World Cup, was ridiculously underrated. The rest of world is beginning to accept now what people have known for years – that this lad is something special. I remember being over at Old Trafford for a visit and men I respect were raving about this young lad. Ken Ramsden and Ken Merritt, the club's secretaries, spoke to me about this youngster who had actually been sent off playing for the reserves. They told me he was a gem. It was wonderful to hear them so passionate about a player. In fact, their boyish enthusiasm was a throwback to Matt Busby's days. Just like in Matt's day, there are now people around Old Trafford who are supporters first and administrators second. In 1994 at Matt Busby's memorial service in Old Trafford I was honoured to be asked to speak alongside Bobby

Charlton, Denis Law, Charlie Mitten and that mercurial Welsh rugby player and broadcaster Cliff Morgan. As I stepped down from the makeshift podium I noticed two ladies sitting in the stand. We knew them as Omo and Daz, the two ladies who worked in the laundry room at Old Trafford. Matt Busby would go down every morning for a cuppa with Jean and Irene, and the players too frequented the laundry room on a daily basis. They were shown as much respect and dignity as the players and that attitude is now, under Alex Ferguson, once again prevalent at the club. Jean and Irene are the mother and aunt of Ken Ramsden and that continuity is also a vital component of a club like United.

Nicky Butt has developed into a wonderful footballer, but Paul Scholes has always been, for me, the jewel in the crown. When I watch Scholesy in action I'm also reminded of a player from another era – Dubliner Johnny Giles. Both had a great football brain, both were great finishers and both liked to, as Danny Blanchflower put it, get their retaliation in first. When I think back to the Milk Cup days, to that wee lad who never spoke two words the entire time he was in Portstewart, it's clear little has changed. He's like Mark Hughes in that respect. I've known Sparky since he was 15 and in the summer of 2002 the organisers of the Northern Ireland Milk Cup asked would I pick him up from the airport. He was guest of honour at the opening ceremony and Bertie Peacock, Hugh Wade and myself travelled down in the car with him. Mark hardly said a word and the following day I joked: 'If you and Scholesy were in the same room together for an hour with 50 people, the next day there'd be 50 people at the doctor's thinking they'd gone deaf.' Mark just smiled back. Paul Scholes continues to live for football, it shows in his game. I get the impression that if he wasn't playing for Manchester United he'd still be out kicking a ball in the streets from dawn till dusk.

If comparisons with former greats are to be made, then I have to say that the closest thing I've seen to the late, great Duncan Edwards is Roy Keane. It's something I've maintained for quite some time and I'm aware that it is regarded as heresy. It may not be a popular opinion with some, but it's true. Keane took over the mantle from Eric Cantona, he became the player to lead by example, the player who could get the best out of those around him. And like Duncan he can defend, create and score. He is the driving force behind United and it was vital after Cantona's departure that someone came along who was big enough to fill his boots.

Of course Roy Keane will now always have to carry the additional baggage of having been sent home from the 2002 World Cup. It's a situation I watched, like everyone else, from the comfort of my living room. I can't comment on his personal relationship with Mick McCarthy, but I can speak about the issues that forced Keane to speak out. The shortcomings in the Football Association of Ireland (FAI) mirror those north of the border – the let's-have-a-few-jars-and-laugh attitude, the moral victories. I remember walking around Wembley before my first international against England in 1957 and some of our officials were talking about how great it was for a wee country like us to be playing there. It didn't matter if we were thrashed by England, as far as they were concerned it was enough to just be there under the twin towers. The things that annoyed Roy Keane were not petty. I can see all the frustration that built up inside him over training facilities and the treatment of the players. Roy Keane's legacy is that maybe now something will be done to sort the situation out. Unfortunately, the whole affair didn't have to happen in the first place. People should be big enough to accept the real reasons for what he started out saying quietly, but which descended into a slanging match with his manager. The country lost out because they didn't have Roy Keane; he lost out because he didn't get to appear on the world stage, but it was no act of self-promotion. Roy Keane doesn't need that. He said his piece because he felt it needed to be said. If it had been handled better, nipped in the bud, or some action taken, then it would surely have not ended in confrontation. The administrators have to realise that without the players there would be no trips. They must always come first.

Roy Keane's teammates also have to shoulder a certain responsibility. They hung him out to dry. I know exactly how that feels. I recall when we were due to play Spurs (the year they did the Double) and I chatted before the team meeting with a couple of the lads. We agreed that the best way to stop Spurs was to stop Danny Blanchflower from pulling the strings. When Matt Busby asked for our opinion in the meeting that's exactly what I said. The boss disagreed; the way he saw it Dave Mackay was the man to watch. I reiterated my point, sitting there praying for the other lads to lend their support as promised. They never opened their mouths and Matt and I ended up in a confrontation. I can't believe there weren't players in the Republic of Ireland squad who didn't agree with Roy Keane.

Now, don't get me wrong, I'm delighted that the Republic of Ireland did so well in the World Cup, but there's something about that homecoming party in Phoenix Park which sticks in my craw. I realise the country wanted to welcome home their heroes, but the bottom line is that they were celebrating the loss of a match against Spain that could, and should, have been won. It was a moral victory and we have got to learn to be above that in the future. I'm not being hypercritical of the FAI. They have done wonderfully well to build on the success during Jack Charlton's reign. And I will also never forget that a few years back when the Republic played the USA they invited me down to Dublin and honoured me with an award. It is something I cherish and is more than I ever received from my own country.

Over the past few seasons there has been speculation in the tabloids that Nicky Butt, Roy Keane and, in particular, David Beckham, are on their way to pastures new. They are still at Old Trafford, not just because of the money and the silverware, but because they regard United, as I did, as their club. Beckham may be a Londoner, but he has a genuine affinity with United. After the World Cup in France when he was pilloried for the sending-off against Argentina, it would have been so easy to swan off to the continent. He could have taken his family to a nice villa, let the dust settle and collect a king's ransom into the bargain. But he didn't. He stayed and stuck it out and I have nothing but admiration for that. I also admire him as a player. I hear people saying that he can't take people on, or can't tackle, he can't do this and he can't do that. In fact, I've had this argument with several of my former teammates. I've seen plenty of players who could tackle, but then gave the ball straight back to the opposition. I've also seen plenty of players who can dribble past six players, but then fail to produce a goal, or for that matter a pass to one of their teammates. Well, I can tell you this, if I was born again I wouldn't come back as a goalkeeper. I'd be a centre-forward with David Beckham supplying the ammunition. Even I could score a bag full. Just consider how many goals have been scored because of his crosses and passes, never mind his ability at free kicks. You have to see the pass to play it. Are his critics going to tell me he's blind as well? David Beckham is an excellent footballer. The lad's got so much going for him. And as for character, you can see that in every game, where it matters, out there on the pitch. One minute he's back behind Gary Neville, the next he's up in attack. He works so incredibly hard for the team. He can lead whatever lifestyle he wants, there's no way you can ever accuse David Beckham of being a prima donna. I'll defend him to anyone . . . he's a helluva player.

Butt, Beckham, Scholes, Keane – each dripping with talent, each with a crucial role to play in the Fergie game plan. But one man thrills me like no other. He alone can make the hairs on the back of my neck stand to attention. Ryan Giggs is the player who can consistently have me on the edge of my seat. From the moment he appeared on the scene I have watched games with one thought in my mind: 'Give the ball to Giggsy.' Like Beckham, he has his critics. Some suggest his end product could be better. My argument is that if you have the ball as often as he does, the law of averages says you'll hit the odd stray pass or cross. I don't want to sound like an old fuddy duddy but the biggest compliment I can pay the Welshman is that he takes me back to the days of the Wizard of Dribble, Stanley Matthews. He is the modern incarnation of men like Matthews, Finney, Lawton, Shackleton – the greats – men who stir the soul. The cold eyes, the deadpan expression, the free-flowing runs with the ball seemingly glued to his left foot . . . Ryan Giggs is what we go to football to see. He is an entertainer.

In 1999 Manchester United completed the Treble. That memorable night in Barcelona they fulfilled the dreams of all Manchester United supporters. They didn't play at their best, but all through that game, to the bitter end, I felt something was going to happen. Maybe it was hope, maybe desperation, but I felt something was going to happen. You see, that's the way it has always been with United. It has always been dramatic.

The history of Manchester United is littered with drama and pathos.

Old Trafford was bombed during the war – then Busby and Murphy came along to rebuild the club, to win the Cup in '48, the league three times in the '50s. Then there was what I believe to be the greatest pool of players ever assembled at a British club – only for it to be decimated at Munich before the potential could be fulfilled. Dark times followed, then Best, Law and Charlton came along to exorcise some of the ghosts of Munich and lift the European Cup. Again the good times gave way to bad, culminating in the travesty that was relegation to the Second Division. And through it all the fans stayed loyal – they would have turned up in their thousands to watch red shirts hanging on a clothes line at Old Trafford. That was a legacy of Munich, whether Martin and Louis Edwards choose to admit it or not. Managers came and went, then the Ferguson era dawned. And just as with Matt Busby half a century before, they told him he would never win anything with kids.

This club and drama are inextricably linked. And I believe in my heart of hearts that there always will be someone, or something, dramatic at Manchester United. That's just the way it is.

XVII

PRIDE AND PASSION

For all emotions that are tense and strong
An utmost knowledge I have lived for these
Live deep, and let the lesser things in life live long.

Those three lines go a long way to explaining the Harry Gregg philosophy.
I don't recall where I read them, or who they were penned by, or even by
how much I may have doctored them over the years. But they are about life
as I see it. Not football. Not Munich . . . life! I was fortunate to be born with
all my faculties, to be blessed with natural and wonderful emotions. The
only thing of real value after that is knowledge.

I feel so incredibly lucky when I reflect on my three score years and ten.
I have learned from great men and played for the greatest club team in the
world. I have lived my dreams.

Two things have filled me with an overwhelming sense of pride . . . my
family and football. The two are also inextricably linked, for the motivation
for my accomplishments on the field of play was the reception back home.
Sure, I got the pleasure of taking part, to say otherwise would be a lie, but
it meant so much to me because it meant so much to my family. More
important than personal pride is my family, who had so little, but were able
to offer me so much. My mother, my brothers and sister, they made it easier
for me. They mean more to me than mere words can express.

I have my own kids (Linda, Karen, Julie, Jane, Suzanne and John) to
thank for allowing me to experience for myself the warm glow of satisfaction
that is parental pride. I can say with all sincerity that playing in the World

Cup, or in the FA Cup final, was no more special than John winning the Irish Cup, or the girls scoring exceptional marks in their music exams. None of them has pursued music as a career, but what others may view as small in the grand scheme of things can assume huge significance to a father. I have always tried to hide my true feelings about Manchester United from my children; it's not in my nature to wear my heart on my sleeve. That said, they all grew up in a home where football was as much a part of everyday life as bedtime and breakfast. The two eldest girls, Linda and Karen, were too young to appreciate my playing days, but they do remember them. Their memories are perhaps of darker times, of accompanying Dad to the treatment room at Old Trafford, of sitting with our physio, Ted Dalton, when I had no one else to look after them. For the younger kids, it is all about my time coaching at United. Playing with Sandy and Sheena Busby's children (Matt's grandchildren), going to the Christmas party at Old Trafford with the players, the staff and their families. I can see them running around that huge empty stadium, up and down the steps, the gloom illuminated by the coloured flares they carried aloft like the Olympic torch. I can see John going with me to The Cliff, playing 'head tennis' with the likes of Ray Wilkins. Or the time he went missing and I found him sitting with Matt Busby having a cup of tea. These are memories I treasure, and, as the years pass, so will they.

Jane and John, in particular, are United fanatics. John, who has enjoyed a good career himself in the Irish League, England, Scandinavia and New Zealand, is far less demonstrative about his allegiance than Jane. She gets so uptight that she can't even watch the matches on television. Instead, she bloody well phones me up during the game to find out the score!

I have enjoyed so many moments of fulfilment during a lifetime in the game. That unbelievable buzz the first time someone asks for your autograph, or when your name appears in the local newspaper. I'll never forget those first few words in the *Coleraine Chronicle*: 'Henry Gregg has been picked to play for the Irish Schoolboys.' I felt as tall as a house. Later my name appeared in *Thompsons' Weekly*, the very paper whose pages I scanned to read about my heroes. 'Linfield Sign Youthful Veteran', ran the headline after I'd played my first game for Linfield Swifts against

Ballymoney United. That cutting is everything to me, every bit as special as any I received with United or Northern Ireland. Occasionally, even now, supporters still recognise me when I'm over at Old Trafford for a match. It's nice to be remembered. At last season's home defeat by Middlesbrough, Bill Foulkes and I were presented to a packed Old Trafford before kick-off. The reception was wonderful. There are moments in time that will never be erased from my memory, like in a restaurant in Germany when the conductor stopped his orchestra, walked over to me in front of the rest of the Manchester United team and said: 'Herr Gregg, *Londonderry Air*.' Those things *do* matter; they are special. And the last autograph I signed? Well, it felt exactly like the first.

I have so many people to thank for their helping hand along the way. When I received my MBE it gave me the platform to mention some of them. I dedicated it to Peter Doherty and the men who lost their lives at Munich. The lads at Munich had further greatness and fulfilment snatched from their grasp, but at least they are still talked about. But if anyone deserved a tribute, deserved to be remembered, it was Peter Doherty. The opportunity to thrust Peter into the public eye was one of the few things about receiving this honour that I enjoyed. I mean, it took until the summer of 2002 before Peter was remembered in any shape or form – Magherafelt Borough Council erecting a plaque on the site of the Doherty home. In the corridors of power at the Irish Football Association, though, there's still no fitting recognition of Peter's contribution.

I recall when the news broke that I was on the 'list'. I took myself off to the Harbour Hill near the Windsor Hotel, in all honesty to dodge anyone who might call to tell me how great it was. Letters arrived from all over the world, they remained wrapped in cellophane until a recent house move. Only then did I take this correspondence out and read it, one in particular intriguing me. I recognised the name, Jimmy Payne, and then it dawned on me. He was Duncan Edwards' best friend. It read: 'You should have had it 40 years ago.'

I know it sounds ungrateful, but my family enjoyed the trip to Buckingham Palace more than I did. I felt uncomfortable in those august surroundings. More than that, I felt unworthy. As I awaited the call to meet

Prince Charles I looked around at men sitting in wheelchairs and thought, 'Harry, *what* are you doing here?' After the ceremony there were four large blackboards on easels held up outside, telling folk that they could have their photographs taken. I didn't avail of their services. In fact, I couldn't get away quick enough. I dragged my wife and children (Linda and John) through the gates. I hailed a cab in my top hat and tails. We jumped in the back and headed straight to the hotel.

Maybe, looking back, I regret not having that picture taken, at least for the family. But that's the way I've always been, always will be. I react to situations. In hindsight there are numerous occasions when my heart has ruled my head, only for me to regret it at a later date. In 1958, after the crash, I was invited to the Yugoslav Embassy. I tore up the invitation. That same year I was also invited to the Player of the Year dinner. I didn't attend. I couldn't go . . . there were people I'd played with who were dead. It's possible I could have been Player of the Year in '58. Like the winner, Bobby Charlton, I'd played again after the crash. Like Bob, I'd helped the club reach the FA Cup final. I suppose the difference was that whilst Bobby travelled to the World Cup, but didn't play, I managed to produce a level of performance that earned me the best goalkeeper of the tournament. At the end of the day, though, I can accept those things. But I cannot say I have no regrets.

The key to life is soaking up all the influences around you, listening to advice from people you respect, and then ploughing your own furrow. Along the way you'll get things wrong, but if you do your best there's no more that can be asked. Perhaps it is another inherited trait, but I've always attempted to pass on the lessons I've been fortunate enough to learn. I know I was a good coach because I was able to tell the same fairy story that had ignited the passion for football in me. If you can hold a player's attention, particularly one who has been hurt, has been told he was finished, useless, then tell him the tale, that is quite a feeling. When a lad's down, you go to him and say you've made the same mistakes in your time. You tell him what he needs to hear. Matt Busby had a masterful knack of saying just the right thing at just the right time. If the press approached him after a match in which you'd starred, he would keep your feet on the ground by saying: 'If you play this game long enough, you're bound to have a good game.' Then, when you had a real stinker, he would defend you with reverse psychology: 'If you play this game long enough, you're bound to have a bad game.' There is something incredibly rewarding about spotting something in someone that others missed, or chose to ignore. It's often just a hunch, a gut feeling that you can mould this man, make him as good as he can be. I've enjoyed moments like that as a coach and I still do. Only last season (2001–02) there was a youngster at Coleraine with bags of ability, but a suspect attitude. I gave him a lift home one night after he'd just heard the manager of the reserve team was dropping him. He was sulking, as young lads do, and I told him he hadn't been dropped, he'd dropped himself. I desperately wanted him to realise that his take on life was going to ruin his chances of ever getting a grip on his football career. Later I also informed him that I'd spoken to the manager. I told him that if I had my time again I could develop this lad into cross-channel material. When I see that spark of real potential, I just can't help myself. I can only hope this young lad learns the lesson.

The call for help can often come from the most unlikely sources. In the early '70s, when the Troubles in Northern Ireland made it the pariah of Europe, teams flatly refused to play there. Jimmy Hill was one of the men who attempted to break the ice. He brought over a team of ex-internationals (including Bobby Charlton, Terry Venables, Bob Wilson and Jimmy Greaves) to play a team of former Irish internationals at Windsor Park. I remember training for a month, getting my own players to shoot at me, such was my determination not to let myself down. The game was a starting point, and in 1978 the late Freddie McFaul phoned me to ask if I would bring my Crewe Alexandra team on tour. Seven years had passed since the last English club set foot in Ulster, but I told Freddie it wouldn't be possible because at that time we could barely afford a bus trip to the local pub. He agreed to foot the bill. I spoke to the players, their families, the secretary and board. And Crewe did tour, staying at The Edgewater Hotel in Portstewart and playing four fixtures (against Coleraine, Linfield, Ards and Ballymena). I will never forget the reception I received from the Linfield fans as I made my way along the track at Windsor Park to the dug-out. Nor the gesture from Linfield's then chairman, David Campbell, who broke with the footballing norm and invited all of the Crewe players into the boardroom after the match. Accompanying us was Crewe's secretary, Ken Dove, and a director, Norman Halsall. During the trip Norman asked me if I knew anyone involved in the farming community. I had no idea what he wanted, but introduced him to John Lynn. I still don't know what these two gentlemen discussed, but a few years later the Milk Marketing Board donated money to the Coleraine & District League, founders of the Milk Cup. And I'm proud to say that one of the mainstays of that youth tournament, now recognised as the best of its kind in Europe, has been Crewe Alexandra.

There are few people who really know me, but plenty who think they do. I might be a stubborn so-and-so, and there's no doubt I occasionally approach things like a bull in a china shop. But there's more to Harry Gregg than this image of an unfeeling, wronged Irishman. In fact, I have never been unfeeling, or felt wronged. Danny Blanchflower had me sussed. He once wrote: 'Harry Gregg doesn't fight, he fights back.' This will come as a shock to many, but I never wanted confrontation.

Pride and passion were the twin pillars on which my playing career was built. I am no different today. My fears for the future of the game haven't dulled my enthusiasm for it. If there's a match on the box, I'll be watching it. In fact, I have been known to lock the gates leading up to the house, take the phone off the hook and pretend that no one's home. Well, a man has to get some peace to watch the game. I am also a proud man and the training regime I still set myself is a part of the very fabric of my being. Age means nothing, keeping active . . . everything.

My attitude to fitness may be unusual in someone who has passed their sell-by date, but not unique. When I was with Doncaster Rovers as a young man I met a former boxer called Bruce Woodcock. A former British heavyweight champion, he had lost a world-title bid to American fighter Joe Baksi, boxing on after having his jaw broken in round one. I used to watch this man who arrived at Belle-Vue in his suit and pork-pie hat. You could tell he once had a powerful physique, even if some of the edges had rounded since he hung up his gloves. Bruce would change in the dressing-room and then run the roads carrying weights. That was not enough, though, and he often did another 30 or 40 laps of the pitch when he'd finished wearing out the tarmac. Bruce Woodcock had long since finished. He was a fight promoter then, but he felt the need to drive himself on. I did eventually pluck up the courage to speak to him one day. An advertisement had appeared in the local newspaper looking for sparring partners for a Tongan heavyweight. It paid £5 a round, and as I was earning £7 a week, I decided to give it a go. I'd boxed a bit as a young man with Coleraine YMCA and the lure of that extra cash overcame all sense and sensibility. I shuffled over to Bruce and offered my services. In fairness to Bruce, he could have thrown me in as a mobile punch bag, but he merely dismissed my approach with: 'Nah, son, it's a whole different ball game.'

I've always followed boxing. I fought as an amateur myself and will never forget reaching a final in Portadown. Control is vital in the ring and I lost it the moment the bell rang. The madder I got, the more my opponent beat me. Eventually the referee stepped in to stop the contest in the third round. I didn't mind getting thumped, but I desperately wanted to go the distance. On the way home I even threw my vest out of the car window. It was covered in blood and I was terrified my mother would see it. Back in my youth I also listened to Joe Louis' fights on a wireless in the Villa Football Club (the only radio in that part of Coleraine). There's something dramatic, almost primitive, about the sport. Two men, one ring, and nowhere to hide. I was fortunate, too, to have met with one of boxing's greatest warriors. I was in New York with Manchester United and received an invitation to appear on cable television. Also on the show was none other than the Manassa Mauler, Jack Dempsey. Now, I know that *nice* and *Jack Dempsey* are not often put together in the same sentence, but that's exactly what he was. In the green room before the show he was charming, with absolutely no delusions of grandeur. I was in awe of the man, yet never felt so comfortable in a stranger's company. Maybe I'm no different to an old prize fighter, maybe I still think there's one more good scrap left in me. I certainly haven't mellowed with age.

At pre-season training with Coleraine in July 2002, I found myself picking up balls that had been kicked behind the goals during a practice game. Suddenly, I thought to myself: 'I'm not here as a ball boy.' I moved onto the pitch and began shouting to a few of the players, just positional stuff, nothing heavy. The next thing I know I've started playing.

Wearing flat-soled training shoes and marking the club's striker Jody Tolan was not a great combination. At one stage Jody moved sharply to collect a pass. He left me for dead and as I tried to make up ground I fell flat on my face. I was angry. Worse was to come. Later Jody went through me like a dose of salts, knocking me unceremoniously on to the sodden turf. I wasn't just angry now, I was livid. After training I went into the boiler room for a quick fag. Coleraine's manager, Marty Quinn, came in and asked if I was all right. Then a worried-looking Jody Tolan arrived, towel around his waist. 'Are you okay. Harry?' I said: 'Why shouldn't I be?' He then started telling me what the players were saying . . . Bang! . . . I was out of there and straight over to the dressing-room. I roared through the doorway: 'Don't f——g collect for a wreath for me!' I laughed about it with Carolyn when I got home. But it also made me realise just what a proud man I am, just how determined I am to kick ill-conceived notions of ageism into touch.

On 9 July 2002, I heard of Ray Wood's death. I had just returned from training on the beach. That morning, a typical summer's one in Ireland, was damp, dank and pretty miserable. I hadn't been in the mood, but nevertheless pulled on a hooded tracksuit top and a pair of waterproof leggings and set off for the strand. I set myself a target in the distance and had only just taken a few strides when the heavens opened. I could so easily have stopped, climbed back in my jeep. But the same thing that kept me going then, has kept me going on a thousand runs before. I thought: 'Your Billy would like to be doing this.' When I got home and my son John informed me of Woody's passing, I considered again my privileged position. As I sat there drying out, I mused on just how much Digger Berry, Dennis Viollet, Jackie Blanchflower or Ray Wood would like to run on that beach now.

The death of a *survivor* inevitably leads to reminiscence. But the melancholy is usually short-lived. When Woody died, I looked out some old photographs, one in particular catching my eye. It was the team climbing the steps to board the *Lord Burghley*, Woody resplendent in his camel-hair coat. I mourn their passing, yes, but more than that I celebrate the life they led. On the beach, in the still hours before the world awakes, I often see their faces. They are all young men. We all are.

THE PHOENIX

(BY HARRY GREGG)

How they laughed, and loved, and played the game together
Played the game and gave it every ounce of life
And the crowds they thronged to see such free young spirits
But, good God, there wasn't many coming home

The dice were cast, for some the last, the final challenge
On a snowbound ground in far off Serbia
The tie was won, the songs were sung, we sang together
But, good God, there won't be many coming home

Roger Byrne, Mark Jones, and Salford's Eddie Coleman
Tommy Taylor, Geoffrey Bent, and David Pegg
Duncan Edwards, and Dublin's own boy Liam Whelan
My good God, there wasn't any who came home

Then Murphy picked the standard up
When all looked lost he made the cut
The fresh young flowers he'd fondly nourished
On a Munich runway had sadly perished

With aching heart he beat the gong
And told the world the Babes lived on
Then Bestie came, he eased the pain
With Charlton, Law, and Crerand

The years between were cold and mean
They never had that feeling
Pretenders came and left again
There wasn't any healing

Then Fergie came and fanned the flames
With Eric's Gallic passion
He gave us Giggs, he gave us Scholes,
He gave us Butt and Beckham

He brought in Keane to lead the team
To even greater glory
My nightmare's gone, my dream moves on
Again I see the phoenix

There are those gone down that long, long road before us
Yet each morn we try and keep them in our sight
In memory's eye the Busby Babes are all immortal
The Red Devil's spirit lives, it never died